Pretty Small

Grand Living with Limited Space

gestalten

Contents

Opaque sliding panels open to reveal the staircase and the raised sleeping platform, as well as providing privacy.

Living Small Is the Next Big Thing

Cheaper to run, easier to maintain, and less taxing on the environment—small-footprint housing is becoming the first choice for people across the globe.

In cities around the world, architects and designers are being tasked with creating increasingly tiny spaces. Individuals, couples, and families alike are losing interest in the scale of properties offered by the suburbs and choosing instead to live in smaller spaces closer to the heart of the urban action.

Choosing to live small is not a new phenomenon. For decades, architects have been striving to streamline the smallest spaces into efficient yet delightful "machines for living," ranging from Le Corbusier's 15 m² (161 ft²) Cabanon on the Côte d'Azur to Kisho Kurokawa's pioneering—if ultimately unsuccessful—effort, the Nakagin Capsule Tower in Tokyo. Throughout the 20th and 21st centuries, skyscrapers and apartment blocks have taken over the urban skyline in conurbations such as London, New York, Shanghai, Tokyo, Hong Kong, and São Paulo, offering small-footprint accommodation to a range of demographics.

As populations continue to grow and land on which to build gets scarcer, rents and house prices have skyrocketed, creating an overheated market that can't meet demand.

Even after the Covid-19 pandemic turned cities into ghost towns, pausing all of their joys and exposing their limitations, the market's upward trajectory has never wavered. The much-maligned office lives on, albeit part time, and the cultural hubbub of restaurants, theaters, and museums in city centers continues to enthrall. Despite all the downsides, people are still prepared to sacrifice space for the thrill of a central location, the buzz of a vibrant neighborhood, and easy access to shops and public transport.

This trend can be seen as part of a cultural shift led by millennials, dubbed the "cheapest generation" by *The Atlantic* in 2012. With the Great Recession in 2007–2009 reducing incomes and job security, and the rise of the sharing economy making everything from cars to clothes available to rent, this generation came of age without their parents' capacity to get on the property ladder, or, indeed, the same interest in doing so.

Instead, this is a generation that values experiences over possessions, and finds jobs that offer a four-day week more attractive than those offering a company car. Similarly, a smaller home that is cheap to buy or rent and maintain, close to both the office and the airport, as well as the social, functional, and cultural amenities of a city, is a more attractive prospect than a larger, more expensive home that requires a commute.

And it's not just millennials. People from all demographics are investigating different ways of living smaller, and their reasons are financial, social, environmental, ethical, and practical. Young people looking for community are finding it in co-living spaces, while individuals looking for something specific are commissioning architects to build it bespoke. Family units are repurposing their garages while developers are snapping up tiny gaps between houses to build skinny homes. In response to the absence of obvious solutions to the dearth of urban housing, architects and designers are creating a panoply of creative innovations that stretch

in Toulouse, with its gleaming white facade and customizable rooms, already looks set to be a classic.

An interesting development in recent years—accelerated by the isolation and loneliness induced by the pandemic—is the increase in co-living communities that offer micro-apartments with access to communal facilities such as gyms, cinemas, roof terraces, restaurants, and co-working spaces. These take the student experience and make it up-market, offering tenants a city-center location at an affordable price with bills included, the flexibility to move at short notice, and a ready-built community of like-minded professionals.

Top Left **Aixopluc's Tiniest House is an easily assembled hut designed to fit inside disused buildings.** Bottom Left **Internal volumes separate the different zones in 8 Tenhachi's Kanagawa apartment.** Top Right **A ladder allows access to out-of-reach cupboard space.** Bottom Right **A view to the kitchen through the window created by a fold-down table.**

Ab Rogers Design's prototype for micro-apartments aims to serve those on low incomes who need to spend up to a year establishing themselves in the city before moving into longer-term accommodation. The property company Noiascape has several small-scale co-living locations around London, each with a different aesthetic, but all offering an affordable communal living and working experience for the short or longer term.

Expectations for a home have never been greater. For better or worse, the past few years have confirmed that the home-office setup is a permanent fixture, and increasingly people are looking to incorporate leisure elements such as exercise equipment, entertainment

and expand the definition of what a house needs to be both functional and joyful.

For many people, their first experience of occupying their own space will come via student accommodation, where single- or dual-occupancy bedrooms offer a modicum of privacy while shared areas such as kitchens and bathrooms help build community spirit.

College life at universities such as Oxford or Cambridge was less about fostering independence in students and more about keeping the young under tight moral and academic control. As universities have moved toward the more cost-effective dormitory model and employed illustrious architects to build their residence halls, student housing has become an important case study for micro-living.

No longer content to be shoved into damp tower blocks miles from campus, students are a voluble and trenchant audience, demanding their money's worth and that their small allocation of space works hard—providing not just somewhere to sleep, work, and entertain, but also storage, access to green space, hard-wearing materials, and a touch of individuality.

Alvar Aalto's serpentine Baker House at the Massachusetts Institute of Technology, where every room has a view of the river, is still the university's most requested accommodation nearly 75 years after it opened, while PPA's recently built Olympe de Gouges residence

tech, and paraphernalia for hobbies, such as books, art materials, and plants.

For those living in smaller homes, this creates a need for intelligent design and smart storage that allows a home to shift effortlessly between work and relaxation. Solutions include computers concealed behind sliding doors, beds folding up against walls, and floors being raised to create storage underneath. Indeed, in a small home, it is not enough for an item to have only one function—to deserve its place it must take on several distinct roles.

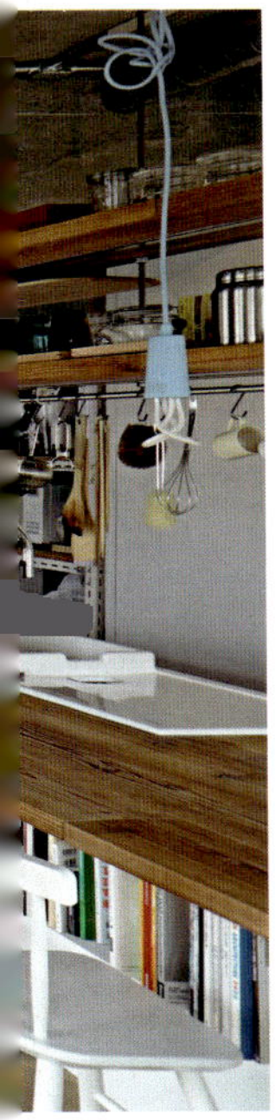

Effective storage is also essential to make small spaces feel spacious, particularly as architects lean toward open-plan layouts to maximize light. Instead of walls, these designs are delineating space using less structural measures, such as moveable kitchen islands, sliding doors, glass walls, a variety of flooring, perforated partitions, and stacked structures, creating visually defined areas without carving up a room.

Employing an architect to optimize a small space for all the vicissitudes of modern life is not a light undertaking, and this can be seen as representing a shift in attitudes to smaller homes. Whether the abode is a Parisian pied-à-terre, a family home in a Mexico City residential block, or a studio for a young professional in Singapore, the effort and expenditure involved signifies a long-term commitment rather than a step on the property ladder. Clients are building their dream homes, expressing their personalities and their passions on a scale that previous generations of homeowners, for whom size was everything, would not have tolerated.

With land at a premium, technology enabling us to downsize our possessions, the environment in a dire state, and the lure of experiences trumping the desire for "stuff," living small looks set to be the next big thing.

A change of floor level and color differentiates areas in Hoa's House.

Living Alone in a Crowd

Not even a pandemic can slow the appetite for city-center habitation, but it has changed how this looks. From micro-apartments to co-living spaces, solo living is starting to look a lot more social.

More and more people—across the developed and developing worlds—are choosing the independence and flexibility of living on their own.

For the affluent, the benefits are clear. Renting or buying a micro-apartment in the city center offers easy access to all the benefits of urban living, from lower rent and proximity to the office to the best in food, culture, and entertainment. Fewer possessions mean more flexibility, greater flexibility in terms of interior design, and more space to cultivate a highly personal vision for living. Privacy is less of a concern and open-plan layouts that blur the lines between work, relaxation, entertainment, and eating spaces are popular.

When interior designer Armando Aguirre moved into a 23 m² (248 ft²) apartment on New York's Upper West Side, he was forced to consider his priorities. He decided a spacious living and entertaining space where he could display his art collection was essential, whereas a double bed was not. Instead, Aguirre designed a custom daybed that converts to a twin-sized bed, which fits into a nook between two closets.

Room Design Buro's client had been inspired by a visit to Hans Scharoun's Schminke House in Löbau, Germany, so the architect worked to bring curves and functionality into a 27 m² (291 ft²) apartment in Moscow, fused with a strongly Soviet constructivist sensibility. Atelier Steve's design for a 22 m² (237 ft²) apartment near Notre Dame combines practicality—curved built-in tables, a mezzanine bedroom, seamless storage, and floating shelves—with glamorous touches such as the rich patina of the timber and an artichoke-green bathroom to create an enviable one-person home.

Proving that there is no reason the smallest space can't be aspirational, Fleur Delesalle turned a 9 m² (97 ft²) space in Paris into a restful bolt-hole using mirrored cabinets, gleaming white floors, extendable surfaces, and a saffron-yellow sofa.

A side effect of increased urban densification and rising land prices is that architects and their clients

Left **A built-in table is the perfect dining space for one.** Right **Curves are used in the shelving and desk, and echoed in the choice of chair.**

have had to use lateral thinking in creating city-center homes. In Japan, London, and L.A., it is increasingly common to see buildings slotted into tiny gaps, creating houses that the Japanese refer to as "eel's nests." One example by YUUA in Tokyo is a 1.8-meter-wide (6-foot-wide) glass-fronted house that stacks multiple levels and spaces into its slender frame. In Quito, Ecuador's capital city, El Sindicato Arquitectura has designed the 12 m² (129 ft²) Casa Parásito (Parasitic House) that can occupy underutilized urban space and provides all necessary domestic facilities with minimal environmental impact.

Of course, there are downsides to living alone. In the long term, single-person households tend to be more expensive, less sustainable, and offer less life satisfaction and security. As urban populations condense and rents balloon, there is a growing concern that only a privileged few can afford to live alone in the city, even as demand for urban living stays strong.

In recent years architects and politicians have argued that housing shortages can be reduced and urban centers regenerated by developing affordable, shared accommodation with communal facilities. In response, a plethora of co-living and communal-living complexes are cropping up around the world. Micro-apartment blocks are nothing new—Kisho Kurokawa's iconic Nakagin Capsule Tower was built in 1972 to provide busy office workers with compact, futuristic pieds-à-terre in the center of Tokyo—but these new iterations are serving a much broader audience.

Top Left **The view from the bed in El Sindicato's Casa Parásito.** Bottom Left **This "eel's house" was slotted into an unused patch of land in Tokyo.** Right **The design creates separate zones by using multiple incremental levels.**

Today's co-living tenants have different demands to their forebears. They are happy to share cooking, working, exercise, and laundry facilities but expect private bathrooms. They want their community to align with their political and social beliefs and priorities, as well as offering experiences that enrich their lives. Ryusuke Anezaki of Swing, the designer behind a compact co-living space in Osaka, Japan, described the benefits to *Dezeen*: "[The tenants] can feel a family-like warmth through their daily life, share cultures, … and help each other when in trouble."

In dense, expensive cities like London and New York, large-scale co-living spaces such as the Collective attract millennials with their central locations, flexible rental agreements, eco credentials, luxurious facilities, and the promise of like-minded fellow tenants. Housing projects such as the U.K.'s Marmalade Lane in Cambridge offer a variety of living options for all demographics, cultivating a multi-generational community centered around shared facilities and social priorities.

Ab Rogers Design has come up with a prototype for a micro-apartment that can be rented for limited periods by those whose income falls below a set threshold. Built as part of a wider ecosystem that offers kitchens,

Top Left **The classic Paris apartment gets an update by Zyva Studio.** Bottom Left **A narrow kitchen is expanded by multiple windows and a skylight.** Right **A balcony canopy adds extra square footage to a small room.**

dining rooms, gyms, music spaces, and communal spaces, the building as a whole would offer each tenant the benefits of a vibrant social hub while their individual apartments remain their own private spaces.

Another take on the multifunctional "home-meets-play" concept is Concrete Amsterdam's blueprint for the 25 m² (269 ft²) rooms at the hybrid hotel Zoku, which are designed for both short and long stays. The brand aims to upend the industry with the cleverly structured spaces, which include a private kitchenette, a desk, and two gymnastic rings hanging from the ceiling, while also offering all the buzz of a city-center location and the convenience of hotel facilities like meeting rooms and a rooftop restaurant.

At a time of increased social fragmentation, communal living is also a way for generations of families to live near each other, maintaining their own spaces while sharing the responsibilities of cooking, caring, and child rearing. In Canada, in Vancouver's wealthy suburbs, former garages and outhouses—known as laneway houses—are being transformed into tiny homes. One example by Campos Studio allows three generations of one family to share a garden and the larger house's facilities while preserving the private space of each group.

Even if the recent pandemic revealed the cracks in an atomized urban system, it's clear that single-person living is not the domain of the unhappily solitary, but increasingly a choice made by those of independent means and defined tastes.

Perhaps in response to a time of enforced solitude and isolation, as well as the relentless upward trend of rent and house prices, the past few years have seen a rise in the number and popularity of co-living and housing projects in urban centers. Individuals—particularly, but not exclusively, the young—are interested in what collective living can offer, be it lower rent, central locations, hotel-quality facilities such as pools, gyms, and cinemas, or community, even if it means their living quarters are small and they have to share a kitchen.

Living as a Couple—Creating Intimacy by Finding Space Apart

Living with a partner in a cozy space can be an intimate adventure but can also amplify differences. What helps are spaces that both connect and separate to meet a variety of needs.

Living with a partner in a nest for two might sound like happiness in a nutshell, but being too close in cramped living quarters can become a source of chronic stress for couples. Having the right mindset can help—our perception of comfort is highly subjective. Good cohabitation practices, such as clear and respectful communication, willingness to compromise, tidiness, and accumulating as little clutter as possible, are beneficial to feeling comfortable together no matter where you live. A well-designed space that reduces the perception of crowding will make shared living all the more pleasant.

Homes that help you inhabit a small space together while maintaining levels of privacy and individuality can help. Athens-based architecture practice SOUTH, for example, transformed an unused basement space in the Greek capital into a 40 m² (431 ft²) custom studio apartment. While basement apartments tend to evoke

images of cramped, windowless, damp spaces, this one, located in the Lycabettus Hill area, is quite the opposite. A sculptural partition wall meanders through the central space, creating distinctive functional zones and various levels of privacy while always maintaining an internal connection. Sensual curves, niches, and cut-outs lend the space a dynamic quality, while arches reach up toward the ceiling for a feeling of added height, directing attention to the two existing skylights. Bright white walls underscore the openness of the space and are complemented by the raw materiality of custom furniture elements in neutral tones, made of unfinished plywood, cement, and glazed ceramic tiles. Functional pieces in black steel add contrast throughout the space.

The reading nook in a Madrid living room serves as a second bedroom, as well as a space to entertain guests.

While the desire to deepen a relationship is a major reason for two people to live together, other factors

may play a role in choosing a snug dwelling for two. Many couples are motivated by necessity and convenience to save money, reduce travel times to see their significant other, and shorten commutes to work or school. Big, bustling cities are appealing for the many opportunities they offer in terms of employment, education, and entertainment, but with high demand comes high rent and smaller spaces. Older couples may have downsized from living as a larger family unit and are embarking on a new phase of life together. Living in a way that is less costly with fewer possessions can free you up to pursue new activities.

When space is tight, clever interior solutions can help make the space work for, not against, you. In Barcelona, furniture designer Max Enrich and his partner, creative director Diana Martin, came up with a number of practical innovations to make their 45 m² (484 ft²) apartment seem larger when they renovated it, including well-placed built-in furniture, a pastel color scheme, and natural light. Their apartment is one of six units in an old 1930s villa in the Catalonian capital. To start with a clean slate, they started by removing the original walls to open up the interior; they now have two rooms shaped and designed to their needs.

The bedroom has built-in storage for clothes along one wall plus an en suite bathroom, where a skylight and window let in light. A space-saving sliding door separates the bedroom from the main room, which combines the functions of a living room, kitchen, dining room, office, and further storage. A wall-length console gives the space a sunny note with its yellow color, while a new cement floor is tinted in sky blue, lending a sense of levity to the home. The kitchen zone, built along one wall, features cabinets up to the ceiling, with a workspace installed alongside it in

Top **The back of the sofa folds up to form a narrow table.**
Bottom **The buttery yellow storage unit holds everything needed in the living room.**

the same design language and pale gray color for seamless integration. An additional kitchen counter-slash-desk folds up from the back of the sofa when needed and can be folded down again to free up space. The dining niche is enclosed with full-length glass windows, giving the impression of an even larger space. If life indoors still feels too cramped, nature is right around the corner—and up a small staircase, where a private rooftop terrace serves as a lush, green lounge area.

A sense of being together yet apart in the same small dwelling was achieved by building vertically in a dense neighborhood in central Tokyo. Japanese studio Unemori Architects designed a house for two on a tiny vacant plot that is very close to the surrounding buildings. The compact house has a 26 m² (280 ft²) footprint, and the architect was able to create a total floor area of 51 m² (549 ft²). From the outside, the house looks like three stacked shipping containers, with a timber framework, cement outer walls, and a facade in corrugated steel, punctured by large windows. Placing the windows on different sides of the building allows light to fill the interior throughout the day and provides a constant connection to the outdoor environment. Inside, the ceiling height of the three different levels varies from 1.9 m (6.2 ft) to 4.7 m (15.4 ft) and there is the feeling of connection throughout the open-plan space. While the interior walls all harmonize in white, a variety of finishes are used to subtly define the different areas of the home. Revealed timber beams and wooden window frames lend a sense of natural warmth.

Top Left **The built-in unit works as stairs and seating.** Bottom Left **Corners create private nooks even in an open-plan space.** Right **Open shelving defines areas while allowing light to flow.**

With limited space, multifunctional furniture can be fun as well as practical. In the 13th arrondissement in Paris, French architecture studio Freaks installed a spinning storage unit at the center of a 30 m² (323 ft²) ground-floor dwelling. Its owners, retired architects who spend most of their time at their home in the countryside, commissioned Freaks to transform a former studio/workshop into a weekend home for urban adventures. The bathroom and kitchen are located at the back of the space, with the bedroom installed as a mezzanine above them; to access it, the agile residents must climb a ladder attached to the wall. Along the opposite front wall by the entrance, low cabinets set beneath the windows provide additional storage. Like all of the other installations, these are white to help the space feel light and airy, complemented by chairs and flooring in honey-colored wood. What truly enlivens the space is its bespoke centerpiece, *la tournette* (the spinner), which has a bookshelf on one side and a fold-down dining table on the other. Not only can the unit be spun around to face in any direction, it can also be positioned to make the apartment feel more open or more cozy as desired.

LIBRE
TAXIMETRO

Family Living— Finding Harmony in Numbers

Family living poses a range of challenges, especially when space is tight. Ideal dwellings are well organized with multifunctional spaces and can adapt to changing needs over time.

Good things come in small packages, they say. But living as a family, especially in close quarters, brings challenges that singles or couples don't necessarily share. Family life generally requires us to constantly adjust to changing needs as everyone grows older, and children move from infancy into adulthood. This includes evolving emotional needs, such as the desire for privacy and intimacy, and also physical needs, such as more space or accessibility issues. Organization is also key, to help manage the accumulation of clutter so typical in today's consumer society. And as the recent pandemic has shown people in many parts of the world, the need to juggle homeschooling and home office can quickly become an unexpected reality. Family living can undoubtedly be a joyous experience, but cohabiting together in a small home highlights a lack of space on multiple levels.

Why would a family choose to live small at all? The reasons are many and diverse. Living in a dense city might bring the benefits of being close to school, relatives, and cultural offerings that everyone in the family can enjoy. And being closer to work means a shorter commute, less time spent away from home, and more time with the family. But urban living often

Left **In narrow homes, creating vaulted skylights also presents space for storage solutions such as clothes lines.** Right **Natural materials help the new house stand out from its older neighbors.**

experiences, which will typically pay less than the salaries they achieve later in their career. On the other side of the generational timeline, grandparents may be living with their children not only to help care for grandchildren but also to be cared for themselves, relieving the burden of the cost of home payments post-retirement.

Left **Three generations fit around this built-in dining table.** Right **A verdant glass-lined corridor creates a buffer between the street and the house's private areas.**

For families investing in a long-term home, a layout that is adaptable to the different phases of the residents' lives can be very practical. In Madrid, Spanish architecture studio BURR transformed a 100 m² (1,080 ft²) space to meet the changing needs of the family who owns it. Occupying the ground floor of a former commercial space, the property consists of two separate dwellings; renting out one of the apartments helped finance the renovation costs. The apartments are separated by a thick, non-supporting wall that serves as an acoustic barrier and can be partially or entirely removed to reshape the space as needed, depending on the future economic resources of the owners

entails having less space that costs the same or more than larger homes that are further away from the city. Whether a financial necessity or a conscious decision, living in a small dwelling can enable families to dedicate more of their budget to things other than housing and avoid having to make the major commitments that go along with owning or renting a larger property. It might also be one aspect of leading a simpler lifestyle: shedding material possessions can help us free up more emotional room for personal relationships and well-being.

Of course, a family can include adult children and extend beyond the nuclear family to comprise a larger constellation of relatives. In many places, young adults live with their parents to save money while completing a university degree or gaining their first professional

or the expansion of their family unit. Storage solutions are installed throughout, particularly in the main kitchen, which makes full use of the high walls. The interior remains in dialogue with the original industrial use of the space, revealing bare bricks, walls, and floors in concrete gray, while simple wood installations underscore the mutability of the space.

Privacy is another crucial issue when there are multiple family members. Having a place to retreat to, however small or symbolic, can provide mental relief for all ages. For a very small family home in a downtown residential area of Nada, Japan, FujiwaraMuro Architects used clearly defined spaces to balance a sense of privacy with the feeling of connection and openness. With the home occupying a 22 m² (238 ft²) footprint on a 37 m² (398 ft²) plot, the architect

found solutions through verticality. The rooms—two bedrooms, a living room, kitchen, dining room, bathroom, garage, and basement storage—are clearly defined through their placement on different levels. A central atrium starts above the ground-level bathroom and ends in rooftop skylights. It serves multiple purposes, bringing natural light into the living areas, providing shelving for storage, and both separating and connecting the spaces, so the very narrow home does not feel claustrophobic. Wooden slats throughout the interior add to the sense of permeability.

Left **A swing creates entertainment without using up precious floor space.** Right **Hanging utensils helps save on storage.**

Togetherness and communication, precious in family life, are principles that Tenhachi Architect and Interior Design underscored when the studio's founders renovated their own 67 m^2 (721 ft^2) ground-floor family home in Kanagawa, Japan. With the exception of the toilet, all of the rooms are connected in distinct and subtle ways. After gutting the interior of the ground-floor apartment, they established one central living area and inserted two large wooden boxes with walls that stop just short of the ceiling. One box contains a sunken bedroom for the parents, with the children's shared bedroom on top of it, accessible by a ladder. The second box contains a bathroom with a rain shower and tub, and a separate toilet. At the heart of the dwelling is a 4.5-meter-long (15-foot-long) cedar table that serves multiple purposes: cooking, eating, working, drawing, and entertaining guests—in short, all essential family activities.

Sometimes, family members might feel too close for comfort to one another. If space allows, this issue

can be solved by constructing a small annex suite, with basic amenities such as a separate bath and kitchenette, or a stand-alone dwelling—the classic images of a teen appropriating the garage as their private domain, the "granny flat," or Canada's "laneway houses" come to mind. Thanks to modern prefabrication techniques, accessory dwelling units (ADU) are gaining in popularity, packing the amenities of a home into a compact space. In Sydney, Australian architect Trias Studio and FabPreFab, a boutique prefabricated housing developer, teamed up to design Minima, a compact 20 m^2 (215 ft^2) living space made from prefabricated cross-laminated timber (CLT). The multipurpose, modular unit can be used as a mini dwelling, studio, or home office. The small dwelling configuration designed by Trias contains a host of practical and space-saving solutions. Its open-plan interior features a bed and a dining table / desk that can both be folded into the wall when not in use, to create extra space. The built-in sofa hides storage beneath it, while discreet shelving wraps around the upper wall space. A skylight in the bathroom brings natural light into the small, enclosed room behind the kitchen. The choice of CLT, made from fast-growing timber, is environmentally friendly and is used not only on the facade but also on the interior walls, floor, and roof, giving the unit a clean, streamlined look. Sliding doors in the same material enable the living area to be closed off for added privacy.

Left **Pull-up compartments in the floor allow easy storage for toys.** Right **Bunk beds allow children privacy in the same room.**

Storage: More Important Than Privacy?

From sliding doors to integrated cabinets, from beds that are couches to bathrooms that become lightboxes; as houses get smaller, exploiting space is getting smarter.

Part of the pleasure of living in the center of a city is that so much of the outside world has been optimized to fulfill immediate desires. Culture and entertainment, food, the office, green spaces—they can all be found beyond the four walls of the home.

In homes with tiny footprints, where finding room for essentials such as beds, seating, and bathrooms is already an elaborate game of Jenga, seamless, often ingenious storage options are increasingly a cornerstone of a client's brief.

More than a kitchen, an entertainment space, or a workplace, home is where one's favorite things are. Therefore, a well-designed house should be an elegant repository for stuff.

The architect's mission to refine storage has been helped by advances in domestic technology, which has been skewing smaller for decades. In the 1970s, Italian furniture designer Joe Colombo created the Total Furnishing Unit, which condensed all the essential services of the home—kitchen, bedrooms, bathroom—into a single complex device. This quite literal take on Le Corbusier's "machine for living in" has been elaborated in the intervening years, as designers insert all-encompassing modular units into micro-housing.

Left The bathroom is lined with hanging space and shelves. Right Arched nooks house elegant open shelves.

Left **Every part of Agius Scorpo's cupboard kitchen has been optimized for storage.** Right **The rear of Freaks' movable unit is made up of storage alcoves.**

A contemporary equivalent can be found in Metre Architects' Gradient Space design for an apartment in Singapore. The flowing timber structure offers "a full spectrum of residential activities" with every element optimized for storage, from the steps that open into drawers to the bed that can be raised to expose a compartment underneath.

Many contemporary designs are taking their cues from far older technology than the 1970s, however, with architects citing boat builders as inspiration for precisely fitted storage solutions. When renovating a 35 m^2 (377 ft^2) apartment in Liguria, Llab Architettura drew on the region's nautical traditions to create a paneled wall of cabinets and doors that concealed two bedrooms stacked like a ship's bunks. By blending storage with the sleeping quarters, the two areas interact seamlessly, occupying a large part of the apartment without dominating the space.

Creating the illusion of spaciousness is the primary ambition of all architects designing small houses. In these pages, this is often achieved by removing light-blocking partition walls to create open-plan spaces where living, dining, working, even sleeping, can all take place without formal separation, as in a hotel room.

But open-plan does not mean that zones go undefined—instead, different elements or structures

inserted a kitchen block with an office-cum-spare room on its roof, complete with a floating desk. For an artist's studio in Paris, Atelier NEA created three floors, including a staircase and sleeping nooks, through the elaborate construction of modular storage units.

Top Left **A piece of artwork on the wall in New York…** Bottom Left **…unfolds to become a dining table-cum-desk.** Right **Contrasting materials stop a wall of cupboards from becoming visually overwhelming.**

In a twist on building up, Sim-Plex added flooring above a deck in an apartment in Hong Kong, which allowed the floor to double as storage.

For materials, architects agree that consistency and light help to create a harmonious environment. Mirrors and reflective surfaces accentuate a space's luminosity. This can be seen in Fleur Delesalle's serene Sevres apartment, where a mirrored wall of cabinets faces an opposing wall of glossy white kitchen units to bounce light back and forth, enlarging the space.

Walls of integrated cabinets designed to blend seamlessly into their surroundings are a recurring feature. In NC Design & Architecture's futuristic Hong Kong home, the identically curved wall panels open and slide to reveal different elements, from a television cabinet and a study nook to cabinets and the bathroom door.

One striking component of the move toward open-plan design minimizes a house's capacity to contain truly private corners, with clients often prepared to be flexible on privacy in exchange for light and

become barriers. COIIO Architecture's filleted gold screen, Tria Arquitetura's perforated concrete, Oriol Garcia's billowing curtains, and Luo Xiuda's wooden cubes discreetly mark off bedrooms and allow light through. In Marn Déco's miniscule Studette apartment, the shift between zones is denoted not by a barrier but in a change of flooring, from wooden boards to patterned linoleum.

Despite taking up minimal space, sliding doors can radically change a room's form. An ingenious design by Agius Scorpo Architects in Melbourne includes a sliding kitchen door that doubles as a room divider to the bedroom. In HCAP's serene Shibuya apartment in Tokyo, a wall of wooden partitions separates the kitchen and bathroom from the open-plan living and sleeping space, creating multiple iterations for space, including a convivial "living bathroom."

Refusing to be limited by floor space, architects working with high ceilings have built upwards, stacking multiple levels into small rooms. Mezzanines are a popular option for bedrooms or storage lofts, easily positioned in the back of a space and away from windows, as in Sam Klemick's L.A. studio.

In some cases the insertions are more dramatic, involving entire structures that house multiple elements. Inspired by Japanese shoji architecture, Proctor & Shaw built a sleeping cube surrounded by sliding translucent screens and positioned on top of a walk-in closet. In Barcelona, Anna & Eugeni Bach

Left **Sliding doors seal off the bedroom from the open-plan living space.** Right **Plywood shelves, cabinets, and drawers form the framework of this multilevel Paris home.**

space. Perhaps this explains the number of glass bathrooms that feature in these pages, such as Studio Bravo's ribbed-glass shower room—by day, a portal for light to reach the bedroom behind, and by night, a decorative feature, a glowing lantern in the living space.

This type of multi-functionality is at the crux of creating practical and sufficient storage in small homes. When every inch counts, every item needs to earn its place, often leading to innovative and highly specific designs in response to the client's brief.

Tasked with making a Manhattan studio feel as spacious as possible, Durodeco responded by designing a dining table/desk that folded away against the wall as a piece of art. Ariel Jacubovich's metal-and-wood staircase winds through a Buenos Aires house and incorporates hanging racks, kitchen shelves, and bookcases. The banister in Studiomama's London town house is wide enough to hold a laptop, while Tsai Design's Victoria apartment is a veritable treasure trove of hidden features, with a folding desk, an office chair that becomes a lounge chair, and a kitchen screen that pulls out to become a dining table for six.

But storage doesn't always have to be about solving the problem of stuff, it can also celebrate it. Max Enrich and Diana Martin's Barcelona home contains a joyous combination of considered built-ins and more eclectic moments, like the Thonet chair that hangs on the wall as art until it is needed for dinner, or the glass display table holding Max's collection of scissors, which doubles as his desk.

Student and Commuter Housing

Students and young professionals are being pushed out of cities by soaring rents and house prices. Could micro-architecture be the solution?

We think often about the weekend retreat: the flight from the city to a rural getaway.

But with more people living outside the city and obliged to travel to work—or who want to keep a place in town for leisure—there is a need for a contemporary take on the pied-à-terre that is small, sustainable, flexible, and affordable.

For students, particularly those studying abroad, the campus living experience is a cornerstone of the university contract. The best examples provide central locations, communal spaces, and personal privacy, cultivating the conditions for a rich and interactive community life.

For these subsets of the population, a portion of their lives is often spent elsewhere, making a small space not just acceptable but desirable. Living smaller does not necessarily mean living worse. It can mean a more streamlined, efficient, even sustainable existence; one with the flexibility to travel at short notice and higher disposable income.

However limited the square footage, commuters and students alike are still looking for practicality, ease, originality, and elegance in their small homes.

In the early 20th century, student housing became a testing ground for new theories of cooperative living, epitomized by Le Corbusier's Swiss Pavilion, built in 1931 at the International University Campus in Paris. Designed in collaboration with Pierre Jeanneret and Charlotte Perriand, it expresses the five principles of the architect's manifesto for contemporary

Left **Green courtyards create extra space in multiperson accommodation.** Right **Using different colors and materials adds interest to identical layouts.**

Left **Mezzanine levels create extra space and privacy.**
Right **Large-scale built-ins allow a wealth of storage in a condensed block.**

architecture—pillars, the roof garden, the free design of the ground plan, the horizontal window, the free design of the facade—which have defined collective housing ever since.

Historically, at universities such as Oxford and Cambridge, students were grouped into distinct houses called "colleges." College life was not unsimilar to a family home, with students housed in a warren of tiny rooms organized as "staircases" and served by a communal dining hall, while their academic and moral progress was kept in order by college staff.

In the 1960s, Denys Lasdun's modernist design for the University of East Anglia's Norfolk Terrace—known as the Ziggurats—marked a radical shift for British students, removing them from the all-seeing gaze of university authorities and allowing them to build a self-defined—and self-catered—unit with their peers.

Ever since residence halls, which are cheaper to run and occupy than the British "college" model, have proliferated on campuses around the world, literally reshaping cities through the architectural interventions and population bump they bring.

Students' needs have not really evolved over the decades, remaining focused on low-cost housing close to campus that aims to cultivate community while protecting privacy. A room has a bed, a desk, storage, easy access to green space, and—ideally—a private bathroom, with cooking, dining, and entertainment taking place elsewhere. The design should have flair but be adaptable to the tastes of different tenants, as well as being hard-wearing enough to endure heavy turnover.

The best examples echo the sentiments of urban planner David Belt, founder of the Macro Sea real estate development firm behind the G27 Global Institute in Berlin: "Our overall approach was to treat our resident students as guests rather than wards of an institution."

PPA's Olympe de Gouges university residences in Toulouse used solid and sustainable materials to create 16 m^2 (172 ft^2) lodgings that "adapt to different lifestyles, cultures, and personalities." Each of the 615 rooms has a long wooden bench that doubles as a desk and kitchen counter, as well as a movable headboard that becomes a sofa cushion. The windows have gleaming white shutters that students can open or close, turning the building's facade into a dynamic landscape.

A smaller example is Hansi Ombregt's student residence in Antwerp, built in the slim passageway between two buildings. With communal cooking, dining, and study rooms on the ground floor, the upper levels offer six dual-level studios, each with huge sliding windows and slightly different interiors. Constructed using robust natural materials and with a design that melds into its surroundings, it demonstrates how students can be discreetly housed within the existing fabric of a city.

While students tend to occupy their accommodations during the semester and leave to go on vacation or return home, commuters are, by definition, constantly moving between locations, creating a need for small, convenient, affordable, and centrally located abodes that can be left for periods of time, or rented out for additional income.

Sim-Plex's renovation of a two-bedroom home in Hong Kong needed to support two parents who frequently travel abroad for work and enlist the help of their son's grandmother for childcare. The architect's solution was to construct a wall of sliding doors that separate the kitchen and living space, turning the latter into an impromptu third bedroom.

For many young professionals, location is more important than square footage. In Taipei, A Little Design was commissioned by a client whose job regularly takes her abroad for months at a time. The architect focused on finessing her 17.6 m² (189 ft²) former piano studio into a functional and elegant bolt-hole where the client could cook, work, and relax between trips.

Similarly, photographer Andrea Wyner travels a lot and spends winters in her native Los Angeles, so her micro-apartment in Milan rarely feels oppressive. "I could not have this in L.A. because you spend so much more time at home there," she says. "Having a European lifestyle where everyone is incredibly social and you can walk everywhere works."

Top Left **Pared-back decoration and simple furnishing maximize space.** Bottom Left **Curtains are an easy way to delineate areas.** Right **A simple kitchen slots under the floating stairs.**

Second homes often have different priorities to those of a primary residence, designed less to express the personal tastes of the owners and more as a launch pad for activities beyond the walls. Pierre-Louis Gerlier's clients wanted their pied-à-terre in Saint-Germain-des-Prés "to feel like a hotel," with minimal storage and only a basic kitchen, as they visit Paris to take advantage of its restaurants.

However, part-time apartments can still be highly specific. Two retired architects commissioned Freaks to turn a former workshop into a place where they could work and entertain during their occasional visits to Paris. Inspired by their clients' work with theatrical set design, the practice created a sculptural cupboard that can move around the space, changing the room's function with its position.

In their different ways, student and commuter housing represent the evolution of modern cities. Soaring rents and house prices have made it hard for students and lower earners to live centrally, yet high-density areas hold their value and their popularity never seems to abate. Affordable, well designed large- and small-scale student housing is proven to enhance learning, cultivate community, and bring income into city centers, while micro-apartments allow young people to get on the property ladder in the heart of vibrant metropolises, prompting cultural and social diversity as well as personal development.

NESTUM
OMO

Work and Leisure

With rising house prices and pandemic concerns, people are increasingly interested in creating multifunctional homes that can be anything—an office, a gym, a cinema, an art studio, even a spa.

Already a preoccupation in modern times, demand for homes that do everything accelerated during the pandemic, and this is just as true in homes with limited space.

When there is no spare bedroom to transform into a home office, architects have to get creative, using intelligent design to create spaces that switch seamlessly between work and leisure. This means incorporating desk space into the existing framework of the house and building dedicated storage that allows computers and tech paraphernalia to be hidden away at the end of the working day.

This ingenuity is not confined to working-from-home set-ups. Clients are also seeking the flexibility to perform more exercise and relaxation rituals in their living rooms. While most small spaces struggle to accommodate stand-alone items such as exercise bikes, architects have incorporated loops into structural beams, so that equipment such as punchbags and gymnastic rings can hang from the ceiling. Projector screens are incorporated into furniture or designed to unfurl from above, and steps are designed to double as seating.

Prioritization is at the heart of designing a small space that fulfills a variety of needs. Increasingly, architects are designing to highly specific briefs, creating tailor-made homes for people with established lifestyles. For many of these clients, small abodes are a long-term lifestyle choice, so they are prepared to invest the money that might once have gone on extra square footage on detailed customization.

For Jack Chen of Tsai Design, the key to creating truly multifunctional homes is ensuring that spaces can "appear and disappear when you need them to," something particularly essential in a 35 m^2 (344 ft^2) apartment in Melbourne. The owner wanted the living room and home office to coexist, as well as a generous kitchen/dining room that could entertain multiple people. The solution was an ingenious wall

Left **Designer Sam Klemick in front of her desk and studio wall.** Right **A simple desk element holds concealed drawers and space for two to work.**

PSYCHIC
OPEN

of concealed storage that holds a desk and computer cabinet for the working day, and then folds out like origami to stow away the work equipment and reveal a large flat-screen television. A similarly inventive retractable screen extends out of the kitchen wall, unfolding to form a table that seats six.

It might not always be possible to hide office accoutrements completely, but some designers have created solutions that put them out of view. In Anna & Eugeni Bach's Barcelona apartment, the installation of a wooden furniture unit to hold the kitchen created space to suspend a desk from the building's exposed beams, creating a useful working area, as well as an innovative design element. In Atelier tao+c's U-Shape Room in Shanghai, the desk sits on an upper level overlooking the living room, its structure incorporated and semi-concealed within the composite piece of furniture that has redefined the whole space.

Louis Denavaut's Paris apartment overlooking Saint-Roch floats a glass desk on a glass mezzanine next to a huge oak-framed window, creating an extraordinary workspace that blends seamlessly with the whole. Sam Klemick's bright L.A. studio makes a feature of her profession, with her sewing table and inspiration wall taking up one side of her small home and most of the furniture being of her own design.

For a 30 m² (323 ft²) home-cum-office in Paris, Bän Architecture was not interested in seamlessly blending work and leisure; instead, the architect wanted to clearly demarcate the two areas. A semi-enclosed kitchen, living room, and mezzanine bedroom is installed to the rear, with nearly every surface painted Yves Klein blue, while up front is an all-white office, complete with plywood desks for three and a Plexiglas conference table. The two spaces share elements—the kitchen countertops have white mosaic tiles while the desk table legs are painted the same vivid blue—but the color contrast ensures the two areas remain clearly defined.

Not every job demands a desk or computer. Abaco's clients in Paris were two actors who wanted an open dynamic space in which to rehearse and perform. The resulting design left most of the floor space open, set the kitchen and sofa into the wall, and set the bed on a wooden platform that could also serve as seating for an audience. A curtain around the bed creates privacy at night while also working as a blank backdrop during a performance.

More and more, small spaces are being fine-tuned to offer everything. Husos worked with a doctor on

Left **Stairs to the mezzanine bedroom hold books and clothing storage.** Right **A raised platform works both as storage and desk seating.**

the renovation of his 46 m² (495 ft²) apartment in Madrid, with a brief that incorporated his regular night shifts in the ER and his heat-intolerant bulldog. The result was a highly specific design that centered around a sleep pod in the living room, somewhere the doctor could nap during the day, thus preserving the bedroom for night rest only. The pod is also useful as a spare room for friends and has a sliding privacy barrier that doubles as a projector screen for showing films.

In Melbourne, Architecture Architecture has gained a reputation for its work in the historic Cairo Flats, where its system of adaptable and fold-down elements allows small spaces to take different shapes according to their inhabitants' demands. The ingenious positioning of all the pieces—desk / table, sofa, bed, storage—within one wall unit means that the shift between work, relaxation, and sleep is a physical one, requiring the literal reformatting of the room to

FASHION
MONET
EGON SCHIELE
Figures du corps
POLINA

Left **Built-in bookshelves and cabinets sit between two identical doors.** Top Right **A standing desk blends in with other storage elements.** Bottom Right **Incorporating a desk into a corner nook minimizes its footprint in the room.**

make it work for the present need, be it working, watching a film with friends, or serving up supper.

Smart furniture is an invaluable method of reformatting space. Black and Milk came up with a six-seater table that shrinks to the size of a console, while the Cini Boeri dining chairs in NCDA's Candy Cube have been put on wheels to make the move between desk and dining area as seamless as possible.

Burr Studio's remodeling of a former office space in Madrid used a series of objects and interventions to dissect the open-plan layout into clearly defined rooms, including a workout space with gym equipment hanging from the beams. In the design for an apartment in Sydney, Nicholas Gurney provided space for his client's interests by incorporating an artist's studio in the central storage pod and planting a miniature garden in the bathtub.

Working from home isn't going away, so the ingenious home office remains top of the agenda for architects and clients alike. At the same time, there is mounting interest in building exercise and relaxation spaces into designs, optimizing dwellings for every aspect of life. National lockdowns reminded everyone that, even in a city, people can't rely on being able to leave their homes to work, relax, or entertain, so it is not surprising that even the smallest abodes are being calibrated to make anything possible inside four walls.

Studette

Studio ______ Agence Marn Déco
Location ______ Paris, France
Square footage ______ 13 m² (140 ft²)

This tiny apartment in Paris's 20th arrondissement has all the elements of an elegantly proportioned and fully functional home.

Designed by Agence Marn Déco as a pied-à-terre for three people, the space consists of an integrated kitchen and seating area, a sofa that turns into a small double bed with a single bunk above accessed by a ladder, and a white-tiled shower room.

Inspired by space-saving measures used by boat builders, the apartment operates like a cabin, with nearly all the furniture built in. The sofa/bed fits under the bunk, its side wall paneled in cabinets, with a rectangular recess holding decorative items.

The bedroom and bathroom are separated by a custom-made frosted-glass window that admits natural light from the bathroom window, while at the same time ensuring privacy.

The slender kitchen is fully integrated, with units hidden behind wooden doors, and a curved white-tiled backsplash echoing in color the rectangular enamel unit above, which in turn mirrors the recess opposite in shape.

Curves are a recurring motif, rounding off the backsplash and the mirrors, and forming the transitions between floor materials, the round marble table, and the splash of blue in the bathroom.

Ignoring the received wisdom that small spaces work best dressed in pale colors, the designer came up with a scheme of deep red,

Left **A bright-blue nook is framed by storage cabinets.** Right **The sofa extends out to become a double bed, with space for a third person in the bunk overhead.**

Left **The slender galley kitchen has built-in seating by the window with a view over Paris.** Below **Bright walls are offset by white details including surfaces and cabinets.** Right **The curves on the vanity unit are echoed in the backsplash, the mirror, and the framing feature wall.**

teal, and Yves Klein blue for the walls, upholstering the seating nook in crimson velvet, setting a bright yellow stool by the table, and lining the bed with lilac linen cushions.

Kitchen and bathroom fittings are picked out in gold, as are the trims on the mirror and the safety bars on the bunk bed. In the kitchen, patterned linoleum takes over from wooden floorboards, the border between the two a thin line of gold.

The overall effect is luxurious and vibrant, diverting the eye without overwhelming the tiny space.

Villa Saint-Michel

Studio ________ Nicolas Bossard Architecture
Location ________ Paris, France
Square footage ________ 50 m² (538 ft²)

Nicolas Bossard's client wanted her apartment to feel like "a cabin by the sea"—not easy to achieve in a 50 m² (538 ft²) space at the top of a historic building in Paris's 18th arrondissement.

Bossard's response was to use every square inch of the limited floor plan, installing a bright and spacious living, working, and dining floor on the lower level, and housing the bedroom, bathroom, and laundry at attic level.

A birch plywood staircase sits at the heart of the duplex, elegantly sparse in its floating construction and taking up minimal room in the airy living room. The back wall houses plywood shelves and cabinets, an ethanol fireplace, and the TV, while behind the front door sits a cozy home office.

Color is used to define and separate zones. Custom-built storage nooks in the living room and bedroom are designed in terra-cotta, while a vivid shade of marigold is used in the desk area and for the arch bridging the living room and kitchen.

Left **The client's primary request was for a separate kitchen, distinct from the living and dining areas.** Right **Floating stairs in the center of the living room take up minimal space and make room for a snug desk area.**

As per the client's request, the fully integrated kitchen is separate from the living room, with storage and appliances concealed behind white and wooden doors. A white quartz countertop is offset by a mirrored backsplash that gives the impression of spaciousness and reflects light, while the exposed brick wall brings texture and history.

A built-in corner bench and table have the seaside feel requested by the client, as well as being the perfect place for breakfast.

Upstairs, the bedroom has a wall of windows to let in natural light from the living room, and the bathroom occupies the highest point under the roof, providing a spacious walk-in shower lined with thin green tiles that were chosen to resemble fish scales.

Clever storage ideas, such as a curved corner cabinet by the front door to house the electrical panel and a closet under the stairs for hanging coats, mean there is not an inch of wasted space, while decorative elements such as linen curtains, pale wood, and glass light fixtures bring the breezy, seaside feel.

Far Left **A painted arch creates a polished feel while distinguishing between two zones.** Left **The mirrored backsplash in the kitchen reflects light and makes the room feel larger.** Top Right **Custom-built storage and wall niches help create an uncluttered feel in a small space.** Bottom Right **The blue tiles in the bathroom were designed to look like fish scales.**

Jourdain

Studio ______ Biloba
Location ______ Paris, France
Square footage ______ 24 m^2 (248 ft^2)

Seeking a new apartment for himself and his girlfriend, Biloba architect Matthieu Torres wanted somewhere affordable, with good natural light.

The couple found a tiny three-room apartment on the second floor of a 19th-century building in Belleville, in Paris's 20th arrondissement. They undertook to open it up, removing every existing wall, closet, and ceiling, exposing the historic beams, and punching three skylights into the roof.

The resulting space provided enough room to install a mezzanine bedroom as part of a compact furniture unit that also holds the apartment's bathroom, walk-in closet, storage, and bookshelves.

Constructed largely from French pine plywood, the built-in unit also incorporates elements that the architect had found or inherited, such as closet handles recycled from Torres's grandparents' kitchen and a cracked bathroom sink that the couple found on the street.

"All these small things are the heart and soul of the space, and are able to express their beauty because of the simplicity of the project," says Torres.

Simplicity, sustainability, and ingenuity are the keywords for the whole project. A folding, movable ladder provides access to the mezzanine bedroom, which is conceived as a cozy, insulated wooden box with shelving.

The tiny, white-tiled bathroom is housed below, with the gold survival blanket used as a shower curtain sending reflections sparkling around the space. Next door is the walk-in closet, with a seat to use when putting on or removing shoes.

Left **A compact furniture unit holds storage, the bathroom, and the mezzanine bedroom above.** Right **Compressing the storage and utilities allows for an uncluttered living room.**

WATCHMEN
JONES
La Bible
TUMULTE
FASHION

Left **The storage unit is built of French pine plywood with recycled handles.** Right **The old workshop table was inherited and acts as dining table, desk, and social center.**

The kitchen is the apartment's main feature—an open space where two people can cook together. The upper walls are kept clear of storage, but there are extensive cabinets below the bench, with door handles made by a ceramicist friend.

"Designing a small space is about choosing what is really meaningful for you, thereby making these functions easy for everyday life," the architect concludes.

LEPIC

Studio ____________ Atelier Baptiste Legué
Location ____________ Paris, France
Square footage ____________ 63 m² (678 ft²)

Positioned under the eaves of an old building in Montmartre, this small Paris apartment offered the interior designers at Atelier Baptiste Legué (ABL) nearly a dozen windows to play with but not much square footage.

They responded by opening up the space, removing all the partition walls to create an airy two-bedroom abode with sightlines that stretch unhindered through the apartment's different areas and out over the rooftops of the city. To add volume, the studio stripped away the existing false ceiling to reveal the building's original oak-beam skeleton.

The beams have been incorporated into the design to lightly delineate the apartment's distinct zones, such as the arch that marks the shift from dining room to living room.

The need for more structural separation between the zones was met with the construction of bespoke furniture, made from resin, steel, and oak, which forms fluid yet functional barriers. The main bedroom is partitioned from the living space by a wall of wide

Left **The historic beams are offset by more contemporary materials, like the stainless steel of the kitchen counters.** Right **A low bench runs around the perimeter of the living room, creating storage and sitting space.**

glass-fronted bookshelves and a soft white curtain for additional privacy, while the kitchen area and second bedroom share a narrower set of bookshelves backing onto the sink and kitchen counter. Using a transparent barrier creates a pronounced division in the space while still allowing light and visual access.

ABL has concealed the bathroom behind a wall of built-in closet space and storage drawers that serve the bedroom. Clad in marble with steel fixtures, the bathroom's open shelving mirrors that used in the living room.

Cooking and entertaining are a large part of the client's life, so the kitchen is open and highly functional, with a large steel island offering plenty of preparation space.

ABL's design for this apartment makes the most of its many windows and long history to turn it into a modern, yet timeless home.

Left **Glass walls create a transparent barrier between the kitchen and the spare bedroom.** Top Left **A storage wall with a pane of frosted glass sits between the bathroom and the bedroom.** Bottom Left **The shower room is clad in gray marble with steel fixtures.** Right **A view through the bedroom into the shower room.**

RAMEY

Studio ____ Atelier Baptiste Legué
Location ____ Paris, France
Square footage ____ 55 m² (592 ft²)

When the client is a chef, it doesn't matter how small the apartment is, the kitchen still has to be amazing.

This was the situation for Atelier Baptiste Legué (ABL) as the studio contemplated the renovation of a 55m² (592ft²) apartment in Paris's 18th arrondissement. Top of the agenda was the creation of a functional and beautiful kitchen space with enough room to prepare restaurant-quality food.

The client also asked for more natural light, which the architect achieved by removing the existing partition walls to create an open space where the windows on opposite sides of the apartment are visible.

Left **A glass wall separates the bedroom from the rest of the apartment.** Right **The kitchen sits in the center of the apartment, surrounded by open shelving.**

ABL positioned the kitchen at the heart of the home, running through its center. The studio created plenty of space to prepare food with the addition of two generous stretches of marble-topped cooking surfaces, and they included extensive built-in cabinets and storage units. Open floating storage, constructed from steel and okoumé wood, sits above, with the pinky-brown tones of the timber echoing those in the marble surfaces. A long stretch of low bookshelves runs along the back of the kitchen while, to the rear, a painted wood shelving unit offers space to display larger objects, as well as elegant camouflage for the pipework running floor to ceiling.

Top Left **Brown okoumé wood complements the streaked brown marble countertops.** Bottom Left **The dining area sits next to the kitchen.** Right **A view down the central kitchen to the glass-walled bedroom and bathroom.**

A steel-rimmed glass wall partitioning off the bedroom and bathroom allows light from that side of the building to enter the rest of the home—with a curtain hung for privacy. The bathroom sink also has a window with a view onto the main living space, but the white-tiled, brick-floored shower has been tucked securely around a corner.

The color palette is consistent throughout: a harmonious blend of whites, creams, pinks, browns, and grays that add a sense of spaciousness to the small apartment.

Point Grey Laneway

Studio ______ Campos Studio
Location ______ Vancouver, Canada
Square footage ______ 52 m² (582 ft²)

With a one-bedroom laneway-style annex in Point Grey, Vancouver, Campos Studio has created an affordable and highly contemporary design to reunify three generations of a family, allowing them to grow up and grow old next door to each other.

Laneways are a type of small building in Vancouver that have gained in popularity in recent years as a response to rising house and land prices in the city's green residential areas. They are named after their location in the alleyways that run behind the main houses on residential streets, with some properties even reimagining their garages to create smaller-footprint dwellings. These can then be rented out for additional income or, in the case of Point Grey Laneway—also known as Miko Laneway—provide multigenerational living for a family with an aging mother, her daughter, and young children.

The family's Japanese heritage was a key inspiration for Campos Studio, as well as the idea that "contrasting elements can make a whole, that imperfection and variation create rather than detract from beauty." The studio also drew on a passion for sailing:

Left **A circular window illuminates the staircase.** Right **The floating staircase enhances the living room's light aesthetic and creates space for seating underneath.**

"We adopted the efficiency of boat building, where elements are asked to perform multiple functions and every available space is used."

Flexible elements include the built-in couch, which works for lounging, sleeping, and storing outdoor gear. Every available space is used for storage, and appliances and mechanical equipment are concealed.

Different areas are marked by changes in flooring material and levels. The entryway is marked by a raised slab, with steps down to the living room's oil-stained concrete floor. Upstairs, the bathroom and laundry areas are denoted by ceramic tiles, with a step up to the smoked-ash floor of the bedroom.

The unusual angular design of the house makes it stand out from other laneway properties, and the exterior black-wood cladding references the trees found in the region's rainforests.

The living space opens out onto the garden of the main house, creating a flow between the two dwellings and emphasizing the connection between the inhabitants.

Left **Dark concrete floors contrast with the all-white palette in the uncluttered kitchen.** Top Right **A simple wood element for storage separates the kitchen from the living space.** Bottom Right **The house is clad in black hand-stained, hand-split cedar shakes chosen for their irregular character.**

Left **The entrance has a double-height concrete slab that can also be used as a bench during parties.** Top Right **Warm white surfaces and gold fixtures create a luxurious feel in the bathroom.** Bottom Right **Ridged frames around the windows turn the outside world into a TV show.**

Hoa's House

Studio ________ IOA Studio
Location ________ Melbourne, Australia
Square footage ________ 104 m² (1,119 ft²)

Left A curved step separates the kitchen from the living area.
Right The house was carefully designed as a showcase for the client's collection of mid-century modern furniture.

A pub, a hotel, an office—at 150 years old, the Kings Arms Hotel in North Melbourne had many incarnations before IOA Studio was commissioned to turn it into a home.

The brief: to transform the old, unloved building into a highly individual three-bedroom home that would also act as a backdrop for the residents' collection of mid-century modern furniture.

The project was highly collaborative, with friends and family enlisted to help rip out sterile office fittings. In the process, they uncovered layers of history and many relics from the building's previous iterations, from cracked plaster to Oregon wood beams and bluestone lintels, all of which were absorbed into the house's new form.

"Small spaces make you work a lot harder to achieve the feeling of space," the architect says. "They demand an intimate knowledge of the site... As the space within is so precious, no part of the project can be left out."

Curved walls were key to hollowing out space, while stripping back the ceiling lining exposed the gable roof. This allowed enough room to create a third floor and bring extra height to the mezzanine.

The architect was particularly proud of the innovations forced by the limitations of the space, such as a pull-out kitchen bench made from recycled Blackbutt flooring and a hidden reading area. Colors and textures delineate different zones, with green and gray concrete floors downstairs in the kitchen and living areas—which can be separated by a velvet curtain—and seagrass carpeting used for the upstairs floors and ceilings.

"We used the small space to our advantage to create warmer, cozier living spaces," says the architect, "while using the colors of the Australian bush to transform a sterile office into an exciting and unique place to be."

Left **A soft curtain provides privacy.**
Right **Painting essential architectural elements, such as the beams, turns them into design features.**

Far Left **Curved Blackbutt walls were the key to designing the space and creating its flow.** Left **Allowing imperfections provides glimpses of the house's 150-year history.** Top Right **Arched storage nooks make the most of otherwise wasted pockets of space.** Bottom Right **Leaving gaps between the tops of walls and the ceiling allows light to penetrate into the house.**

Left **Seagrass matting covers the floors and ceilings upstairs to tactile, cozy effect.** Top Right **A third floor was created by removing the original ceiling lining, opening up space for the main bedroom.** Bottom Right **A skylight illuminates the top-floor desk area.**

The Warren

Studio ____________ Nicholas Gurney
Location ____________ Sydney, Australia
Square footage ____________ 49 m² (527 ft²)

Renovating a small Sydney apartment for a client who is a committed and unapologetic accumulator of art and objects, Nicholas Gurney's priority had to be storage.

His solution was to build a large storage hub capacious enough to hold all the client's clothes, a laundry, an art space, a pull-out bed, and bookshelves.

This took the place of the main bedroom's partition walls, which were removed to allow light and air to move freely through the space. The bedroom was repositioned in the former bathroom—a narrow nook just large enough to hold a queen-sized bed—and the bathroom was situated in the former laundry.

The storage pod serves to define zones within the new layout, separating the bedroom and bathroom from the more public areas, as well as creating a niche that doubles as an art studio and a spare room—with guests given privacy by a thick curtain stored in the pod that can be pulled across the entrance.

By cladding the pod in mirrored gold, provided by Italian company Abet Laminati, the architect turned it into a dynamic force in the apartment, creating luminosity and reflections, and amplifying the effect of the trees and plants that are placed on every surface. Plants even find their way into the bathroom, where Gurney designed

Left **White walls are the backdrop to the client's eclectic collection of colorful furniture, art, and plants.**
Right **Windows on both sides flood this small Sydney apartment with light.**

a soaking tub and shower with a miniature garden installed at one end, so his client can enjoy nature even while performing his ablutions.

All the appliances are integrated and concealed to create a fully functioning kitchen that doesn't intrude into the rest of the space, with wall space left free for art.

The client plans to live in the apartment for the foreseeable future, continuing to accumulate objects to display and enjoy. Gurney's design works to create a luminous backdrop for living, making, growing, and collecting that will continue to function for many years to come.

Far Left **A central storage pod clad in mirrored gold acts as a double-sided room divider and "store-all."** Left **Salmon terrazzo tiles cover the floor.** Top Right **A mustard velvet curtain can be drawn across to transform the art studio into a guest room.** Bottom Right **Plants everywhere make a house a home.**

Top Left **Part of the bathtub has been given over to create an indoor garden.** Bottom Left **The storage pod holds a double bed, which can be pulled out when needed.** Right **The mirrored gold creates a radiant, cocooning effect in the small bedroom space.**

The fully integrated kitchen is clad in gold and blends discreetly into the design.

The Greek Apartment

Studio ______ ABACO
Location ______ Paris, France
Square footage ______ $42m^2$ ($452ft^2$)

ABACO maximized all available space in a small apartment in a 1990s Parisian building to create a singular home for two actors.

As performers, the clients needed the living room to be open and dynamic, with furniture and functions designed to fit snugly into the boundary walls, leaving a stage for their practice.

The principal furniture elements are united in a single, unique piece of oak furniture. At the rear is the bathroom, constructed as a self-contained wooden box with a hidden door. This is the first element of the structure that leads into the apartment's main room to form the platform for the bed and runs along the wall to the window as an integrated storage unit holding the kitchen and reading niche.

On the opposite wall is a piece of undulating plastic that contains concealed closet space, floating shelves, and a large painted frame that serves as a home office or small dining table.

The clients were less interested in privacy than in freedom of movement, so the studio is conceived as a communal space where working, relaxing, performing, eating, and sleeping can all take place without strict boundaries. The bed's platform doubles as both a stage and seating area, and a lime-green curtain—concealed in a nook in the oak unit—is available to encircle the bed and provide a barrier if needed.

The architect was inspired by the clients' Greek heritage and chose to infuse the home with the colors of their homeland—the traditional bright-white paint found in Greek architecture and the blue of the Aegean Sea.

While the oak unit creates a coherent structure on one side of the apartment, the white plastic wall opposite plays many parts. Filled with hidden storage and dotted with specific items including coat racks, books, and the clients' beloved record player, perhaps most vitally "it acts as a screen to diffuse the light" with the angle of its ripples precisely measured to best reflect the sun's rays during the day.

Top **An oak block houses all the functional elements of the apartment.** Bottom Left **A huge window ensures the open space is flooded with light throughout.** Bottom Right **Fixed elements on both walls contribute to the flexible, open-plan layout.**

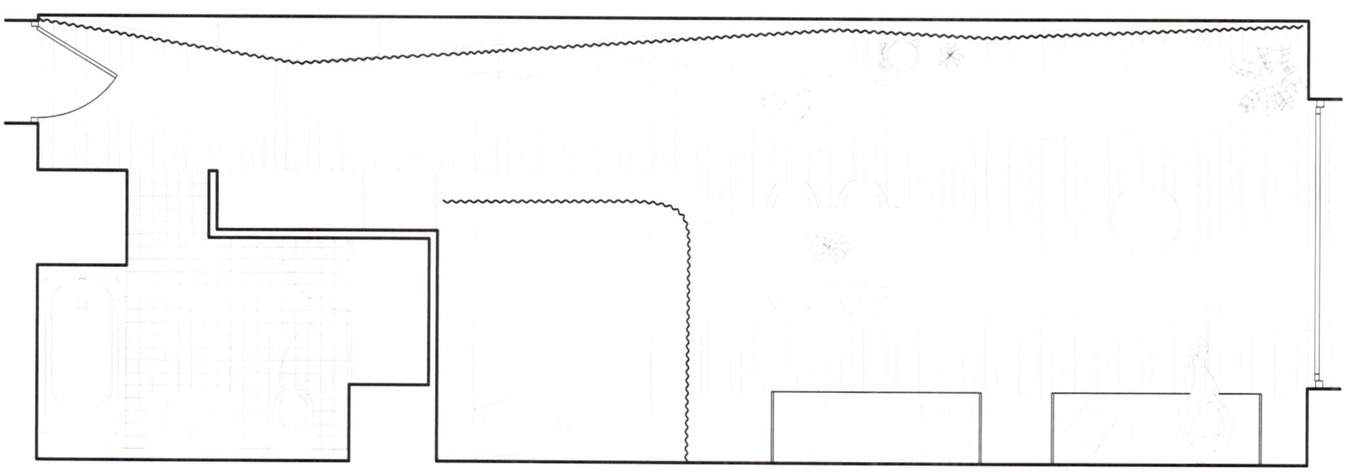

Top Left **A plastic undulated wall adds dynamism while concealing storage.** Bottom Left **A curtain can be pulled across to separate the bed from the integrated kitchen.** Right **Floating MDF shelves hold books and the client's beloved record player.**

Pilon

Studio ________________ Helft & Pinta
Location ________________ Paris, France
Square footage __________ 60 m^2 (646 ft^2)

A ground-floor apartment in an old Paris building was given new life and light through an energizing renovation by local practice Helft & Pinta.

Working in close collaboration with the clients, a pair of graphic designers, the architect reconfigured the space, demolishing a central wall to allow light to flow into every corner of the apartment from the courtyard on one side and the garden on the other.

One of the client's requests was for a large glass wall featuring oak wood arches. This feature became the wall of the bedroom, keeping the private space separate from the rest of the dwelling while still allowing daylight through to the living room.

The bedroom is designed to be a haven, with a reeded wooden wall holding a storage recess, and thick curtains that can be pulled across for privacy.

Arches are a repeated motif throughout the apartment, repeated on doorways, storage niches, curved mirrors, even sink basins.

Top Left **The arched entry alcove creates space for cabinet storage.** Bottom Left **Foxed mirrors bring texture and reflections to the bright kitchen.** Right **Arches proliferate throughout the space and are echoed in the curves of the furniture.**

Left **The oak-framed glass wall allows light to flow from both sides of the apartment.** Right **White zellige wall tiles and porcelain fixtures are warmed by the terra-cotta floors.**

While the dominant color is soft white, other tones and textures have been incorporated to draw the eye and demarcate different zones, such as the rich red on the living room entrance arch and the hexagonal tiles in the shower.

The fully integrated kitchen has IKEA units paneled in BauBuche wood and cupboards covered in foxed mirrors, which bring a gentle abstraction to the functional space while making it feel larger. The living room furniture is tactile and rounded, echoing the arches in the design and adding to the sense of comfort and ease. The apartment is filled with cleverly concealed storage, ensuring the space remains peaceful and uncluttered.

"The project strives to enhance the impression of country life," says Helft & Pinta, which used natural materials like terra-cotta, wood, and whitewashed stones to cultivate an elegantly rustic spirit in contrast to the frenetic urban energy outside the walls.

Apartments HKS

Studio — Hansi Ombregt Architectuur
Location — Antwerp, Belgium
Square footage — 25 m² (269 ft²) each studio

In the university quarter of Antwerp, Hansi Ombregt Architectuur was tasked with transforming a tiny plot of land that had previously been the passage between two buildings into comfortable, spacious accommodation for six students.

The resulting design created a statuesque block finished in black slate with large red-rimmed windows, featuring six dual-level studio apartments, all with the same essential layout but finished in different styles and materials.

The glass-fronted ground floor is communal, with a large kitchen and dining room, as well as a multifunctional study space. The six studios occupy the three floors above, two on each floor, facing either the street or the rear courtyard.

Despite the tiny 25 m² (269 ft²) footprint, each studio stacks its bedroom on a plinth above the washing and cooking zones, leaving about 15 m² (161 ft²) of open, flexible space for sitting, eating, and working, lit by the huge sliding windows that fill almost

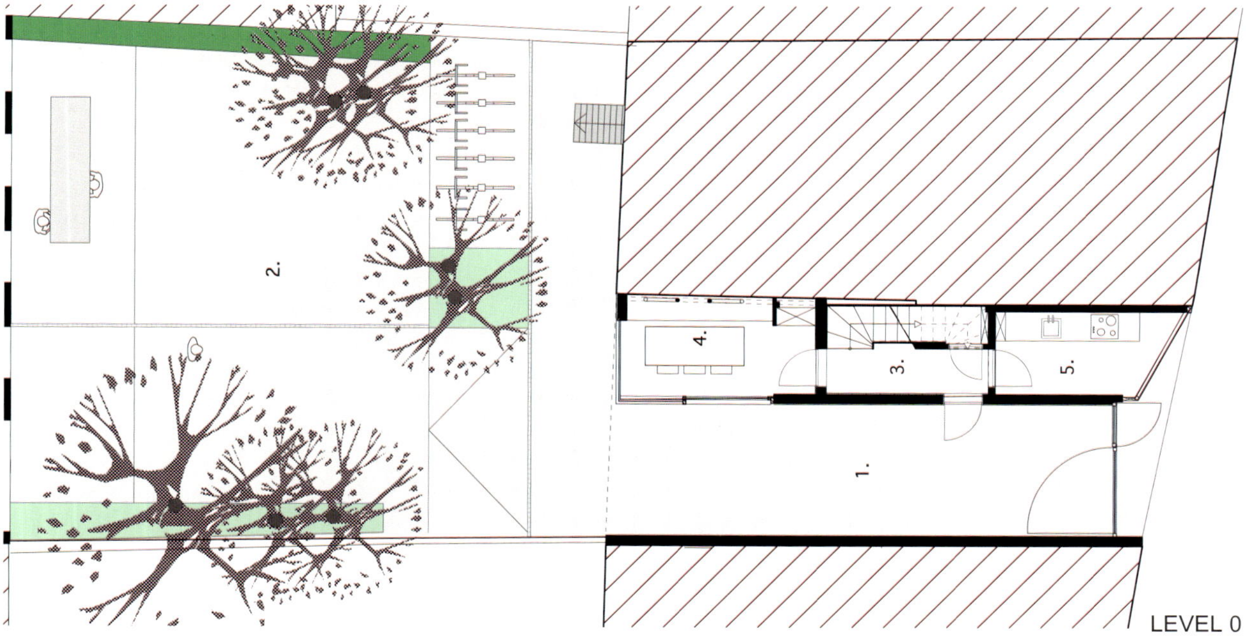

Top Left **The apartment block is slotted into the former passageway between the neighboring buildings.** Bottom Left **A tree-lined courtyard to the rear has seating and bike storage.** Right **A multifunctional communal area with tables for working or eating sits on the ground floor.** Bottom Right **The communal kitchen has floor-to-ceiling windows overlooking the street.**

the entire wall. The rooms feature some storage, such as a drawer under the platform leading to the mezzanine stairs, but tenants are left free to organize rooms according to their taste.

Clever construction of the building itself, which sits on a steel frame and directly abuts the external wall of its neighbor, not only makes the most of the additional space that would have been taken up by an internal wall, but also turns the original bricks into an interior design feature.

Student housing throws up specific challenges as spaces need to be flexible, robust, stylish, and inexpensive, and equipped to deal with a high tenant turnover. To meet these considerations, the architect used raw materials such as old bricks, concrete, and steel, which look timeless and are extremely hard-wearing. They also allow the new building to slip seamlessly into a historic city environment, appearing clearly as fresh and new, but not contrasting egregiously with its neighbors.

Above **Simple MDF shelves provide extensive desk space and open storage.** Top Left **Each of the six apartments has large sliding windows framed by the black slate facade.** Bottom Left **High ceilings create space for a mezzanine bedroom accessed by a ladder.** Right **The bathroom sits behind sliding doors opposite the compact kitchen.**

Left Here a slightly different layout has the bed jutting out on a plinth. Above The simple desk extends above a stretch of white drawers. Below Each floor has the same basic layout, but each studio is finished in a different style, using different materials. Right The cut-out steps leading to the bedroom blend into the wall behind.

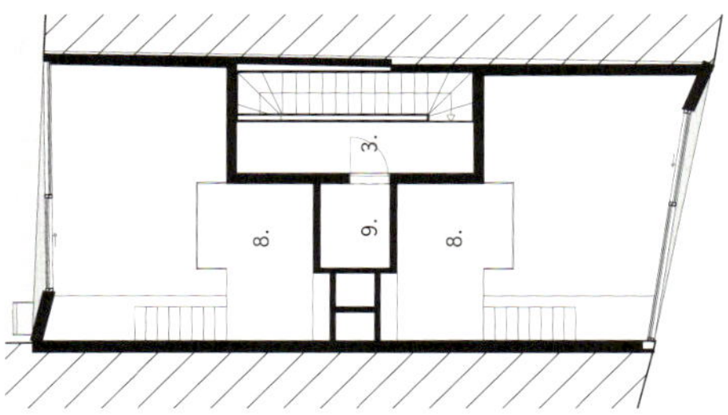

LEVEL +3 duplex

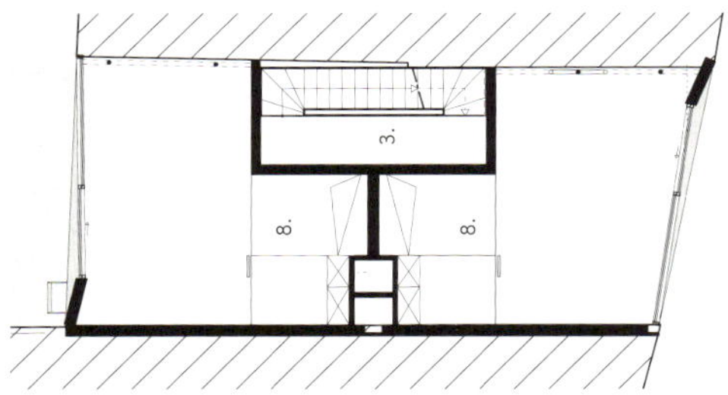

LEVEL +1, +2 duplex

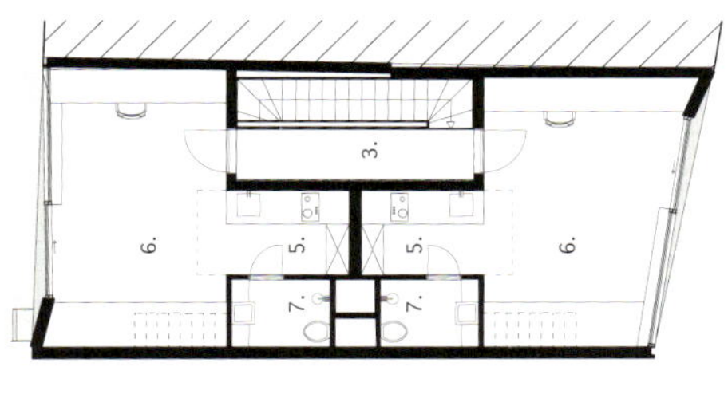

LEVEL +3

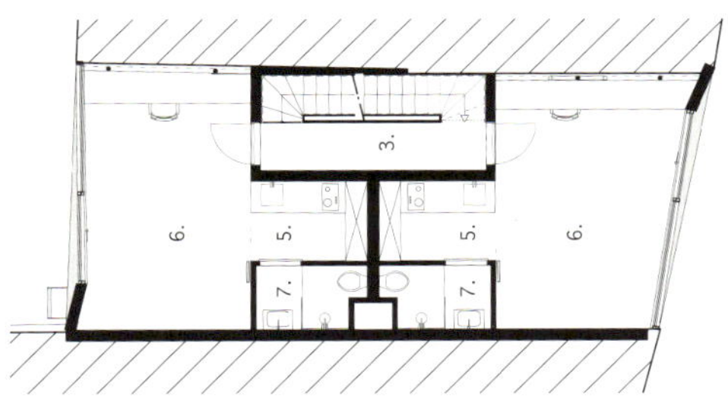

LEVEL +1,+2

Studio 1

Studio __________ Agius Scorpo Architects
Location __________ Melbourne, Australia
Square footage __________ $23\,m^2$ ($248\,ft^2$)

This apartment in Melbourne's historic Cairo Flats building was a personal project for the architect pairing of Claire Scorpo and Nicholas Agius to create a home for Agius himself.

The U-shaped block in Melbourne's Fitzroy district was designed in 1936 by Acheson Best Overend and considered strikingly avant garde for its time. One of the city's best-known architectural landmarks, the building has largely kept its structure of mostly studio apartments built around a central garden, showcasing Overend's ethos of "maximum amenity at minimum cost and space."

The architects wanted to maintain this credo as well as updating the space for modern life. They came up with the idea of a "crafted tool chest in which to sleep, eat, and wash"—a creative living space that could be used for many different purposes while allowing two people to coexist with privacy.

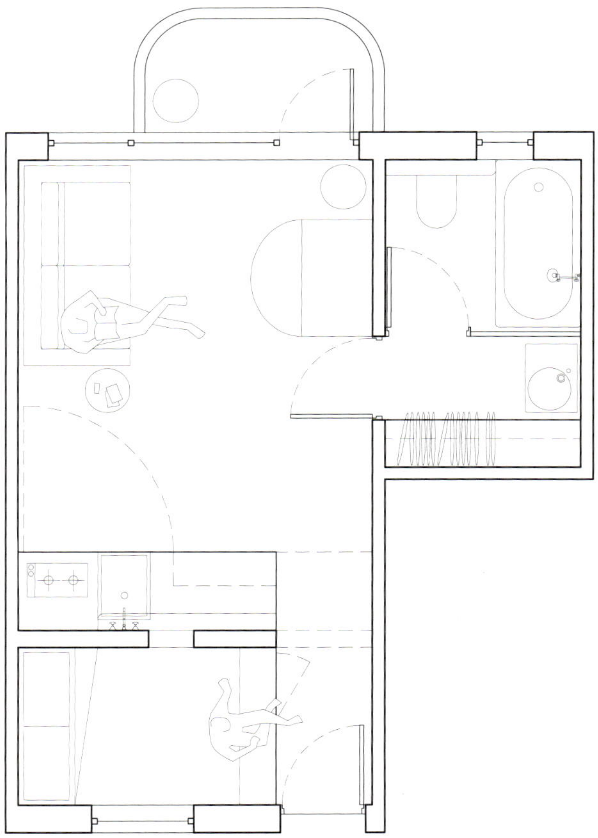

At the heart of the apartment and its functionality stands the kitchen cabinet, a robust and multifunctional construction inspired by traditional woodworking benches and built from recycled Victorian ash hardwood. A large hinged door and a smaller sliding one open to reveal the kitchen surfaces and appliances. The inside

Left **Sliding doors create private zones within a small space.** Right **Bright color makes the kitchen door a design feature as well as storage.**

of the larger door doubles as a pantry, while the smaller one can be pulled across to separate the bedroom—formerly the kitchenette—from the rest of the apartment.

Another example of hybridized walls can be found next door, where the bathroom and closet areas are separated by a corrugated glass partition that doubles as a shower screen.

Most of the apartment is painted bright white but Agius pays tacit homage in his use of bright yellow for the kitchen details to the bold hue used by Le Corbusier in his Côte d'Azur seaside getaway, the Cabanon de Vacances.

Left **View out onto the apartment's small balcony.** Right **The kitchen door fits seamlessly to conceal the entire unit.**

Top Left **Floor-to-ceiling fluted glass allows light to flow from the bathroom.** Bottom Left **A view from the living room into the compact open closet.** Right **Raising the bed creates a storage vault underneath.**

El Camarín

Studio IR Arquitectura
Location Buenos Aires, Argentina
Square footage 25 m² (269 ft²)

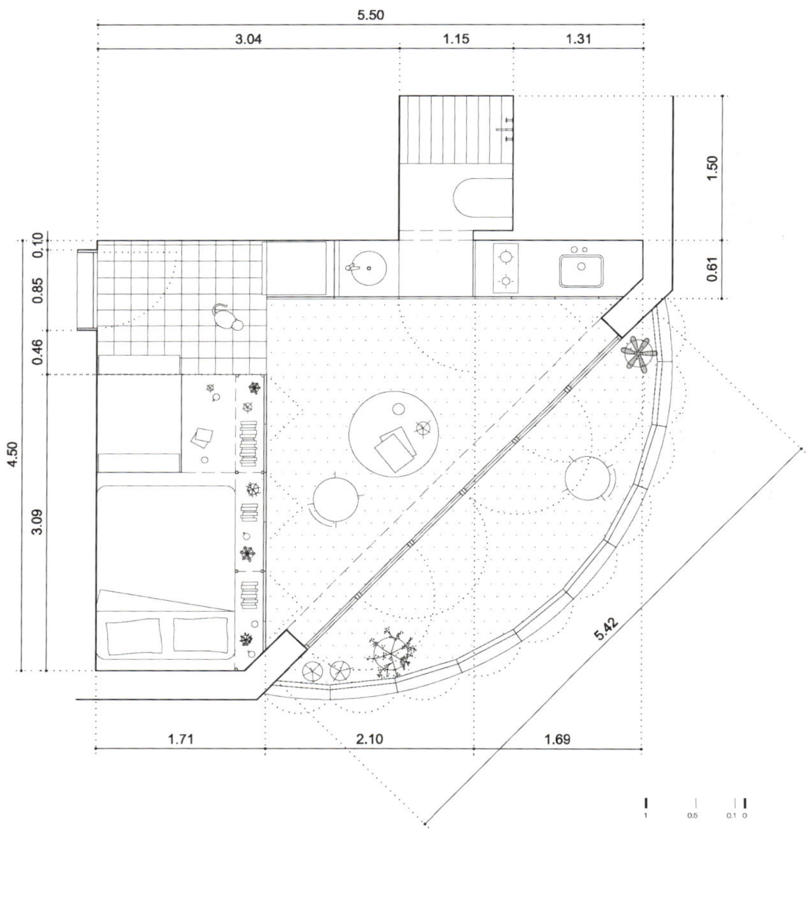

Proving that no space is too small to be transformed into something innovative and habitable, IR Arquitectura turned a forgotten corner of a 1950s building in Buenos Aires into a tiny apartment.

The triangular dwelling, dubbed El Camarín, is in the district of Chacarita, to the north of the city center. Its eye-catching exterior features a scalloped balcony designed by the practice to add an extra 7 m² (75 ft²) to the original floor plan.

Curved white mesh sections let in light and allow the residents to look out, while obscuring the interior from curious eyes. A glass ceiling ensures the space is filled with light, while folding glass doors can be closed to shut out any draughts during the winter months and opened up in warmer weather. The architect describes the addition of the terrace as "a diaphragm able to expand the use of the apartment in summer and to contract it in winter."

The rest of the space is an exercise in maximizing a tiny footprint. Built-in furniture forms the two principal internal walls. On one side is the small kitchen, with cabinets concealing appliances, a folding table for eating, the stovetop, a sink, and the door to the

Left **Incorporating the balcony added 7 m² (75 ft²) of extra space to the tiny floor plan.** Right **A wall of white cabinetry conceals the bathroom door.**

bathroom. On the other side is an open bookcase and shelving unit that partly conceals the bed, a desk, and cushioned bench, while still allowing light through.

To increase the sense of both light and space, walls are painted white and the flooring is sleek concrete. Color is added through pot plants, red accents on the shelves, and bright blue door knobs on cabinets.

IR Arquitectura describes the apartment as an ochava, meaning chamfer, in reference to the shape of the original space and the position of the building on a chamfered street corner. The apartment makes a striking addition to a growing repertoire of small homes carved out of unexpected or forgotten spaces.

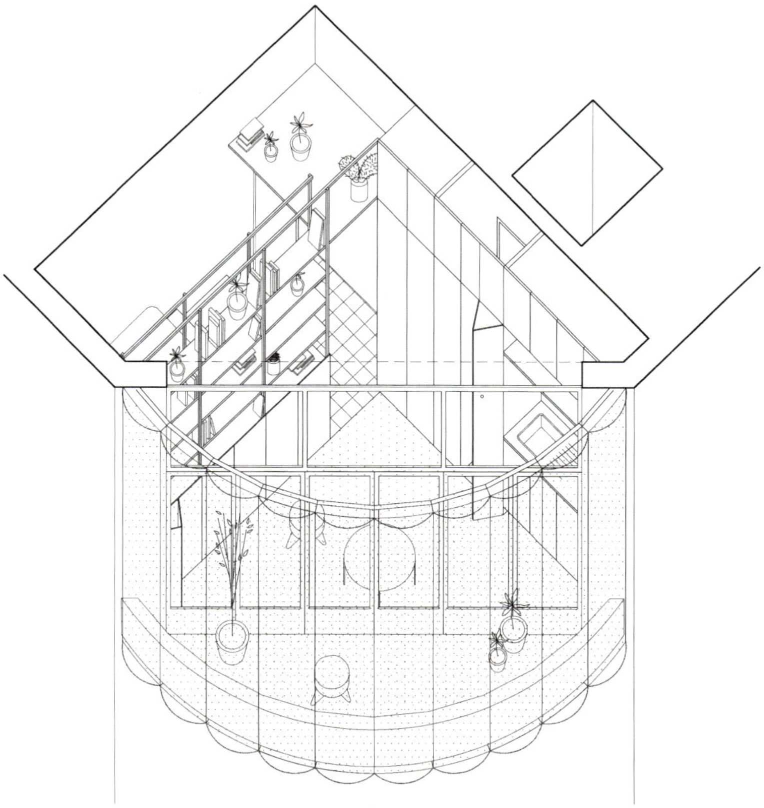

Top Left **Open shelves gently separate the bed and seating nook from the rest of the apartment.** Bottom Left **The balcony's scalloped edge is an eye-catching feature both inside and out.** Right **Folding glass doors keep in the heat during the winter.**

MICRO
Information Graphics

Information Graphics

Left **A small dining table unfolds from the kitchen wall.**
Right **A ladder provides access to the high-level cabinets.**

The balcony's mesh enclosure allows light in while maintaining privacy.

U-Shape Room

Studio	Atelier tao+c
Location	Shanghai, China
Square footage	42 m² (452 ft²)

Atelier tao+c was tasked to transform what had once been the ballroom of a 1930s building in Shanghai's French Concession district, designed by modernist architect Robert Fan, into a contemporary and flexible living space for a young couple.

With one wall dominated by a huge bow window, the room boasted natural light and high ceilings but no separation of space. Atelier tao+c countered this through micro "furniturization," an approach that reimagines architectural objects as complex pieces of furniture. The studio inserted a large composite structure into the room to keep the original walls, windows, and ceiling intact while accommodating disparate living areas in their own independent zones.

Top Left **The plan shows the scale of the composite furniture object that creates the levels and storage in the room.** Bottom Left **The bed floats out over the room on a plinth.** Right **Different levels create privacy and a sense of separation within a small space.**

Made of maple plywood, the structure incorporates all functional requirements, including a shower, closets, bookshelves, desks, stairs, and beds. Details from the ladders to the guard rails and kitchen counters are picked out in painted metal and stainless steel, while purpose is delineated with different floor surfaces—white ceramic tiles for the bathroom, and terracotta tiles, commonly used in Shanghai parks, for the ground floor and leading into the garden. There are no partition walls, allowing light to reach deep into the house and illuminate every nook. Despite being a single-room dwelling, the different levels create privacy, and a separation between the public and the private. The upper level, which can be reached either by a wooden staircase or a metal ladder, has an office area and a floating bed cantilevered out into the center of the room on a plinth. The space above the front door is left open, creating a full-height foyer and enhancing the connection between the two levels.

Top Left **The end of the bed doubles as open shelves.** Bottom Left **The bathroom is tucked into the furthest corner of the room, near the entrance door.** Above **A chair in the same maple plywood as the larger structure.** Right **Terra-cotta tiles line the floors in the social areas of the home.**

Kerry Hill
LE CORBUSIER LE GRAND
Japan Living
PROJECT JAPAN

A simple plywood bench mirrors the arc of the huge bow window.

Tsukiji Room H

Studio ______ Yuichi Yoshida & Associates
Location ______ Tokyo, Japan
Square footage ______ $47\,m^2$ ($506\,ft^2$)

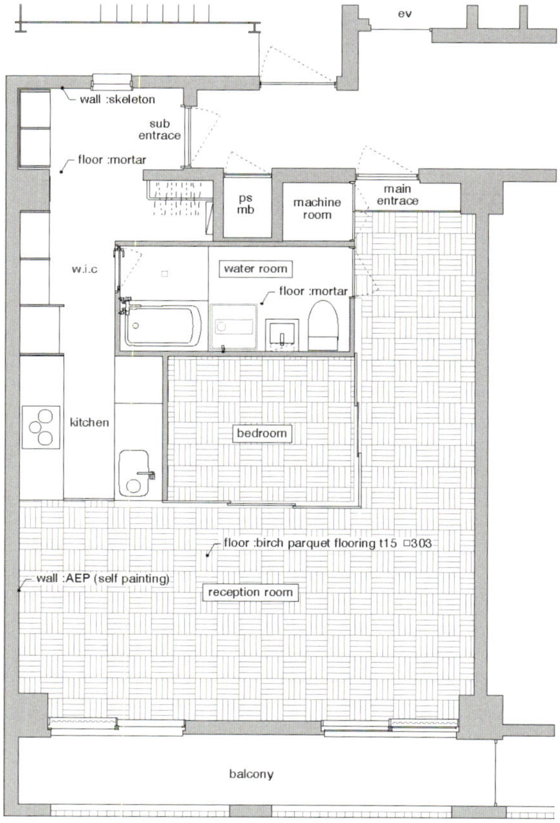

Yuichi Yoshida & Associates' renovation of a former office space in central Tokyo is an exercise in forward thinking.

The client wanted to create a living space that would be their home for the next 5 to 10 years, after which time they planned to sell it or rent it out. They commissioned the architect to create a simple open-plan apartment that works for day-to-day living and can be easily subdivided to serve different purposes, thus emphasizing flexibility and spaciousness over individuality.

A wooden box was positioned at the center of the apartment to house the bedroom, with one wall forming the side of the narrow galley kitchen and the opposite side forming the entrance hall.

The bed sits on top of a platform of storage drawers, and the whole area can be concealed behind sliding wood doors to ensure privacy at night and to transform the reception room into a formal working area during the day. A small white bathroom is next to the bedroom, and a walk-in closet and utility area sit at the end of the kitchen.

Left **Grouping all services and storage in the back corner allows maximum light into the living spaces.** Right **The double bed sits on a plinth of storage drawers abutting the bathroom wall.**

Decorative design interventions are minimal yet informative, emphasizing the temporary, raw energy of the apartment while also aiding functionality.

The concrete walls have been left with their plaster corrections still visible and the apartment's metal piping has been left exposed on the ceiling. The kitchen has stainless steel surfaces and plasterboard shelves suspended from metal rods. The floor transitions from concrete in the kitchen and bathroom to a pattern of light wooden tiles in the living room, denoting a zonal shift from the functional to the public space.

The living room is open and mostly clear of furniture, with the exceptions of the hammock hanging by the sliding glass doors to the terrace and a large dining table that also serves as a home office. These are all temporary items, however, in line with the client's desire to create an undidactic space that a new owner or tenant can fill with their own vision.

Top Left **The open-plan layout enables flexibility, with the dining table doubling as an office space.** Bottom Left **Sliding doors conceal the bed from view during working hours.** Right **A large hammock turns one side of the room into a leisure space.**

Shoji Apartment

Studio ________ Proctor & Shaw
Location ________ London, U.K.
Square footage ________ 29 m^2 (312 ft^2)

For the architects at Proctor & Shaw, the commission to renovate a cramped apartment in North London became both an exercise in innovation and a rebuttal to the idea that size is everything.

"True quality of space, no matter how big or small, matters," the studio says, and Shoji Apartment demonstrates that a beautiful, functional home can be achieved with a smaller footprint than 37 m^2 (398 ft^2)—the U.K. government's minimum space standard for the floor area of new homes, as given in its technical housing standards.

The new design dispensed with the second-floor apartment's existing layout of cramped rooms, removing partition walls and exposing the huge bay window at the front. While floor space was scarce, the ceilings soared to 3.4 meters (11.1 feet) high, so "by exploiting the vertical dimensions, space is conjured out of nothing." The architect added an innovative sleeping pod comprising a king-sized bed raised up on a wooden plinth that is accessed via a plywood staircase, with a walk-in closet below.

Top Left **The design creates extra living space by stacking rooms and storage.** Bottom Left **Soft clay plaster walls complement the pinkish sheen of the birchwood joinery.** Right **Concealed lighting transforms the sleeping pod into a dramatic design element.**

Left **Sliding polycarbonate screens reveal the stairs to the king-size bed above.** Top Right **Floating shelves provide storage for art and photographs.** Bottom Right **A view into the walk-in closet under the bed.**

The pod is surrounded by a series of sliding translucent screens "inspired by Japanese shoji screen architecture, which create a 'sleeping cocoon' that animates the living space through different configurations." Not just a sanctuary, it is also a striking design feature, with internal lighting enabling it to act like a lantern and illuminate the entire space.

A fully integrated kitchen with floor-to-ceiling storage runs along one wall of the apartment, while the walk-in shower room has a structural ceiling that creates space for loft storage above.

Soft clay plaster on the walls and ceiling chimes with the joinery's natural birchwood, the polycarbonate screens, and the flooring's functional linoleum, creating a harmonious and spacious whole.

"By designing 'compact,'" the architect summarizes, "greater attention is directed towards material qualities to bring delight back into the spaces we inhabit. The project highlights that quality is more important than size, and innovative design beats generic rules-based solutions every time."

Shibuya Apartment 402

Studio — Hiroyuki Ogawa Architects
Location — Tokyo, Japan
Square footage — 34 m² (366 ft²)

In the renovation of a one-room apartment in Tokyo, Hiroyuki Ogawa Architects deliberately set out to create an extreme contrast to the busy city outside the window.

While Tokyo is fast paced and frenetic, Shibuya Apartment 402 is serene and spacious, a large white space that can be transformed into different zones using the central panel of sliding doors. Built from naturally textured wood in a distinctive zigzag pattern, the screens play a dynamic role in allowing the inhabitant to take control of the space, to find peace, privacy, and relaxation.

The main room has a domed ceiling and windows on two sides, with an airy atmosphere that is accentuated by the absence of built-in furniture. This room can take on any role, from bedroom to dining room to living room, its plaster walls and tiled floors making it a blank canvas.

On the other side of the room, the screens pull back to reveal an unusually large bathroom with space for a shower, a vanity unit,

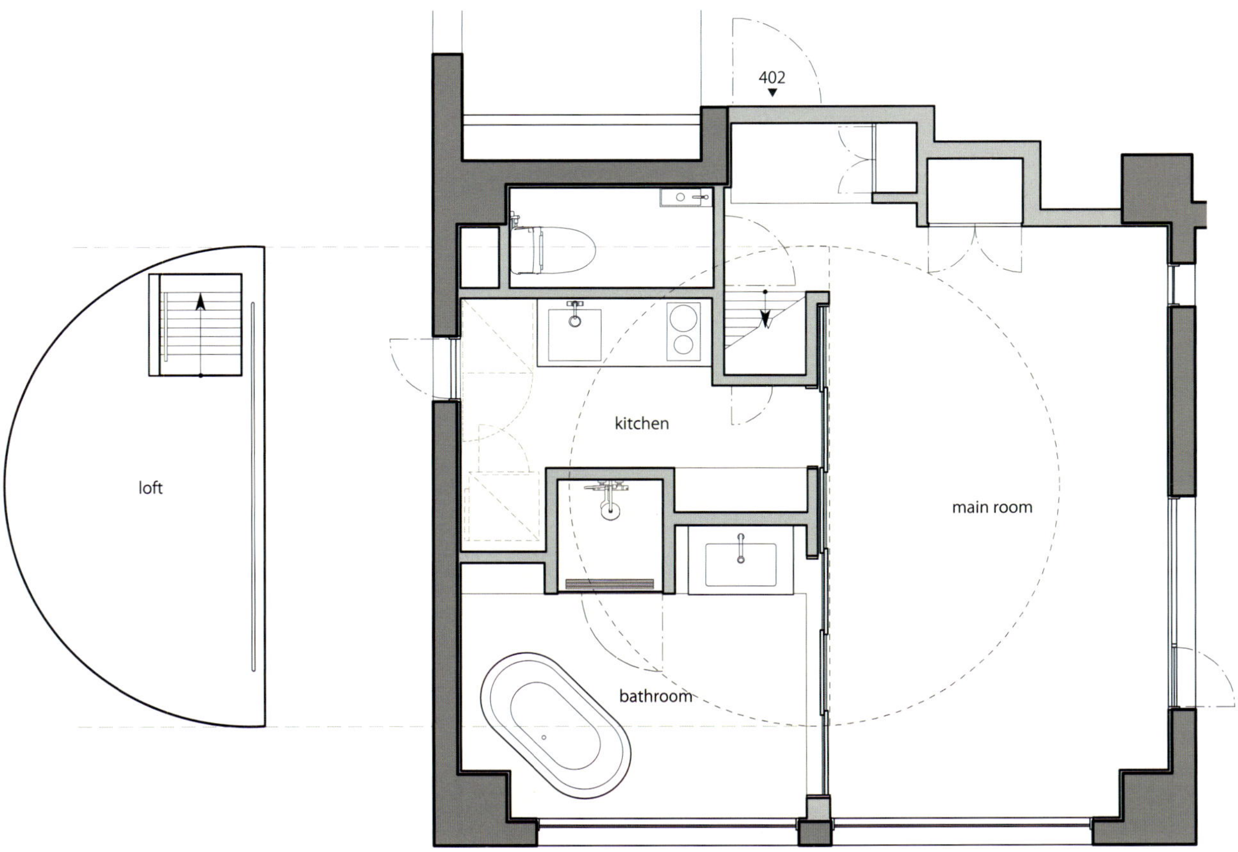

Left **The compact kitchen is slotted behind the bathroom.** Top Right **The loft space acts as a light well, forming a dramatic design feature.** Bottom Right **Sliding doors separate the bathroom from the main room.**

and a huge soaking tub positioned with views out of the floor-to-ceiling window. "When connected to the main room, the possibility for such activities as reading, enjoying a film, or having a cup of tea turns the space into a 'living bathroom,'" says the architect.

The kitchen, adjacent to the bathroom, is also concealed or revealed by the central screens, and both rooms sit beneath the loft, a storage space with a domed ceiling. A striking architectural element by day, at night the dome becomes a dramatic light feature, softening the lines of the room and adding to the calming atmosphere.

Most architects choose to make the bathroom the smallest room in the house. For this apartment the practice chose to bring it front and center, creating the perfect haven for the busy city dweller who prioritizes performing their ablutions in a tranquil, beautiful space.

Top Left **Simple, luxurious fittings line the back wall of the bathroom.** Bottom Left **A bath with a view.** Right **The view from the bathroom into the main room.**

Straight Curves Apartment

Studio ____________ Zyva Studio
Location ____________ Paris, France
Square footage ____________ 50 m² (538 ft²)

Working both with and against the historic heritage of his surroundings, architect Anthony Authié of Zyva Studio created a mashup of old and new in this apartment overlooking the Matignon gardens.

"Two eras. Two styles. Two colors. Two floorings. Two shapes. The project emulates a game of ping-pong that leads us from one element to its exact opposite," says Authié.

While taking care not to eradicate the Haussmanian elements that define nearly two centuries of Paris architecture, Authié blends them with his own contemporary, computer-generated tastes.

The living room is as close to conventional as the architect allows, leaving the original period floorboards, cornices, and creamy walls largely intact. However, it's the details that matter. LED light fixtures form fluorescent echoes of the historic ceiling cymas, while the furniture—a slumped Philippe Nigro sofa in bright blue, a triangular table with 3D-printed legs, and a neon orange rug by Louis Lef—work together to render 19th-century tastes a distant memory.

Off the living room, the angular kitchen is all glossy white lacquer except for blue faucets described as "an ode to Raf Simons and Sterling Ruby's shirt," blue light fittings, and a curtain that appears flame-licked. Next door a curved space holds the bathroom, decked out in deep-blue mosaic tiles that create the feeling of diving into deep water. A curved cabinet holds two sharply rectangular sinks and more blue taps, while a mosaic door conceals the rest of the bathroom fixtures.

The bedroom, a simple space with thin, ceiling-height closets on either side of the bed, is dressed in flame-themed fabric designed to emulate computer-generated particles.

With its heightened aesthetic and oblique historic references, Authié's singular design for a small apartment manages to take a brightly colored journey into his computer's algorithm while keeping its feet firmly on the ground in Haussmann's Paris.

Top Left **View of the living room.** Bottom Left **Open shelves house objets d'art above and curve downwards to form storage niches.** Right **A chain tapestry by Wendy Andreu hangs by the entrance.**

Left **A squashy Philippe Nigro sofa sits on an orange rug by Louis Lef.** Right **The white kitchen is enlivened by the blue faucet, blue light fittings, and a flame-hued curtain.**

Left **The royal-blue bathroom creates the feeling of being immersed in water.** Right **The restored moldings are a reminder of the apartment's Haussmannian heritage.** Top **Faucets by Martí adorn stainless steel sinks.** Bottom **The bedroom appears engulfed by flames.**

NN06

Studio	Burr Studio
Location	Madrid, Spain
Square footage	100 m² (1,080 ft²)

Burr Studio was commissioned to transform a former office in northern Madrid into a minuscule yet fully functional one-bedroom home. Without altering the previous configuration, the architect reimagined the space using a novel visual and material language, creating two "families" of contrasting materials—metal and wood—serving different purposes.

The studio drew a distinction between the immovable aspects of the building and the more moveable elements—the furniture. This was defined through materiality and color, stripping back the surface coverings of ceilings, floors, and walls to lay them bare, with the bright-blue metal structural objects designed to fit into openings or hang

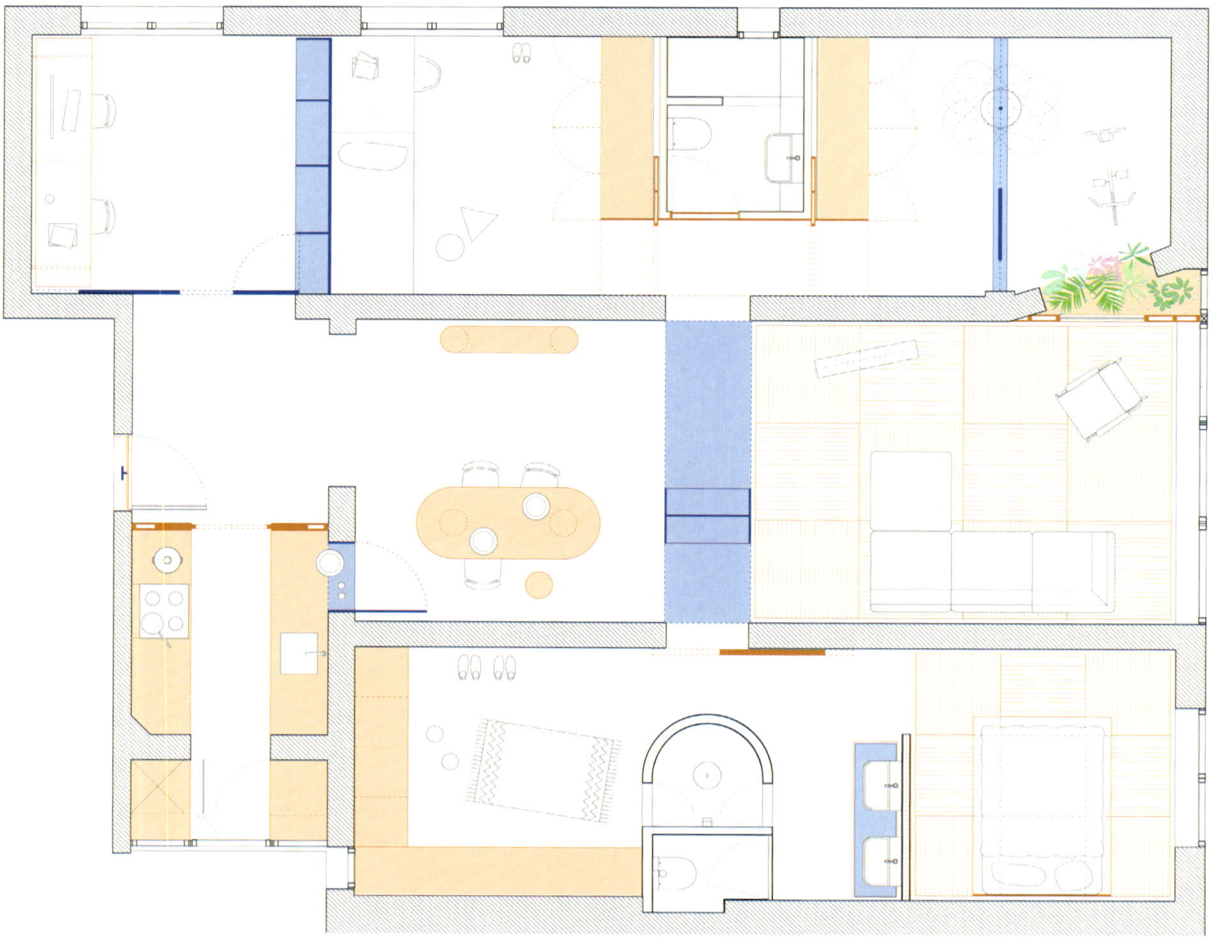

Top Left **A mirror and shelves in the hanging element create an elegant entrance hall.** Bottom Left **The plan shows the blue metal "plug-ins" that allow the inhabitants to use the space in different ways.** Right **A view from the workspace.**

from beams, such as the T-shaped bookshelf at the center of the apartment. This has been designed as a functional object, a room divider, and as a totem that the various activities of the house take place around.

Other elements of the metal furniture are also suspended above the ground, adding lightness to their physicality, as well as referencing their temporary nature. They include a gate that separates the workspace from the domestic area, an interior shutter to isolate the kitchen, and an exercise beam.

In contrast, the wooden elements rest on the pre-existing floors, which were stripped back to give them a raw, elemental character. Plywood platforms add height and a degree of separation to the more intimate spaces, such as the bedroom and the living room, while functional areas such as the kitchen, bathroom, and storage cabinets use the clean lines and ease of wood, mirrors, and ceramic tiles.

Together the elements combine to showcase Burr Studio's design ethos of intervention that leaves no trace, featuring movable elements that can be discreetly reconfigured, and making for a highly individual, multifunctional home tailored to work, leisure, relaxation, exercise, and creativity.

Left **The hatch in the kitchen opens out over the dining area.**
Right **The central bookshelf delineates zones as well as providing storage.**

Left **All the metal elements hang, suspended above the ground.** Right **An internal window brings light into the workout room.** Top Above **A beam has dedicated hooks for exercise equipment.** Top Below **Plants and foliage proliferate in the corner.**

Saint-Roch Duplex

Studio	Louis Denavaut
Location	Paris, France
Square footage	70 m^2 (755 ft^2)

Interior architect and designer Louis Denavaut was commissioned to renovate and decorate this Parisian duplex on rue Saint-Honoré that boasts a staggering view of the dome of Saint-Roch Church.

Home to two artists, the redesigned space celebrates the apartment's original features and provides an elegant, modern backdrop to the classicism of the skyline.

Antiques and works of art are mixed with bespoke, tailor-made items. In the living room, a huge circular window puts the dome center stage, and custom-built bleached oak banquettes with leather cushions are positioned to make the most of the view. Underfoot are the geometric lines of the original parquet floor, while suspended overhead is a round sculpture whose curves mirror the window, opposite.

Shapes, textures, and materials echo each other throughout the space. The glass mezzanine floor has a pale wooden seam, and the combination of wood and glass is also found in the coffee table, as well as the large oak-framed skylight and the desk that sits beneath it.

Also featured in the mezzanine is a steel railing inspired by vintage ocean liners, its stark framework reflected in the tubular chairs and the legs of the 1970s Italian table below.

The kitchen and bathroom are adjacent on the lower floor, with the fluted glass of the bathroom enclosure playing off the rippled marble that forms the sink and culinary workstation. In the bathroom, glinting black zellige tiles cover the custom-made bath and walls, under a matte black ceiling.

Wood, glass, steel, and marble are the dominant material elements, set against bright white walls and rare spots of color; this muted, refined palette draws the eye to the view outside.

"The aim of this project was to open up the space by bringing in as much light as possible," says Denavaut. "As in an airplane, we follow the course of the sun, we see the clouds go by… in summer when there is a storm, it's magic."

Top Left **Built-in bench seating overlooks the dome of Saint-Roch Church.** Bottom Left **Steel frames act as banisters.** Right **A round sculpture hangs in place of a chandelier.**

Left **Glass on glass on glass in the desk area.** Right **Steel details abound throughout the apartment.**

Top Left **The kitchen is simple, with wooden cupboards and a marble countertop.** Bottom Left **Glossy zellige tiles add sensuality to the bathroom.** Right **Reeded glass walls keep the bathroom private.**

Left **The neighboring dome in all its glory.** Right **Carefully chosen antiques work within the limitations of the historic building.**

AFR Koszutka

Studio ____ Mistovia
Location ____ Katowice, Poland
Square footage ____ 35 m² (54 ft²)

A small apartment in Katowice's design district was given a facelift by Mistovia to make it an eye-catching addition to the rental market.

Perfectly positioned on the 11th floor of a 1970s block in the center of town, with views of the Silesian Museum and the International Congress Center, the apartment was redesigned to make it stand out from the preponderance of bland, neutral rental properties on the market.

Mistovia created a striking visual language, using rich colors and vibrant textures, that paid homage to the apartment's 1970s heritage while also staying within the client's strict budget.

Removing most of the partition walls turned two small rooms into one open-plan space, with a kitchenette opposite the curved bathroom enclosure by the entrance leading into the bedroom and seating area.

With just a single window, Mistovia found innovative ways to keep the space bright, such as building the curved wall of the bathroom from glass tiles—also a nod to the building's modernist heritage. Stainless-steel cabinets bounce light off mirrored doors and surfaces, and one wall has been stripped back to its original concrete.

Left **Curtains extend from the window to surround the corner storage cabinet.**
Right **Every surface is different, from raw concrete and steel cabinets to glass tiles and mirrored walls.**

Mistovia also incorporated bright colors and soft textures, with the sleeping area featuring red curtains and a velvet headboard, the plywood bathroom door painted a vivid teal, and densely patterned terrazzo chosen for the kitchen and bathroom floors.

"Taking inventory of the apartment, we found perfectly conserved furniture polished to the point of shining," Mistovia says. "We decided to use them, giving them new, surprising functions—the chest of drawers has become a kitchen cupboard, a cabinet now frames the television." A mix of vintage and modern furniture—Paged bentwood chairs, a geometric table, a refurbished crystal lamp from local store Szpeje—combine to create a singular, highly engaging interior that ensures the apartment stands out on any rental site.

AFR Koszutka

Left **The living and sleeping zones are delineated by a shift in flooring materials.**
Right **A nook houses the TV and a mid-century cabinet found in the property.**

Modernist Estates
RADICALLY MODERN
Openhouse
Issue Nº10

Top Left **A blue-stained plywood door leads to the shower room.** Top Right **Terrazzo lines the walls and floor while a mirror extends up the wall across the ceiling.** Bottom Left **Glass bricks give the room a distinct 1970s vibe.** Right **The pared-back sink and stove top blend almost unnoticeably into the design.**

Gran Via Apartment

Studio ________ Anna & Eugeni Bach
Location ________ Barcelona, Spain
Square footage ________ 70 m² (753 ft²)

A young couple recruited Anna & Eugeni Bach to renovate an apartment in an early 20th-century building in the Eixample district of Barcelona.

The brief was to maintain the existing two bedrooms, with their charming balconies at the facade, while finding room in the remainder of the small space for a kitchen, living room, bathroom, and work zone.

The solution was found in the soaring ceilings. The architect added a galley kitchen, constructed as a distinct box, to the apartment, with its roof creating a loft area that doubles as an office space—complete with a floating desk suspended from the original wooden beams—or a spare bedroom.

The kitchen design freed up the central space for a living area and dining room, and it is also an access point to the other rooms in the apartment. The kitchen was carefully designed to offer

Top Left **The new plan keeps the two bedrooms as before while opening up the living space.** Bottom Left **A floating desk makes the most of high ceilings.** Right **View from below to the kitchen ceiling-cum-office.**

maximum storage and includes innovations such as a folding table that provides an additional surface for food preparation and a wide hatch-like opening into the dining room.

The bathroom also provided scope for ingenious space-saving solutions. Elevating the floor not only created additional storage but also allowed the bath to be concealed underneath the shower tray, combining both functions in a single spot.

As expected from an older building, the apartment was full of historic features that the architect was careful to maintain and celebrate. The original wooden beams, doors, and window frames were left untouched, and the new features, such as the kitchen and floating desk, were also made largely from wood, though in a paler, more modern variety.

By utilizing the existing features of the apartment, the architect was able to find extra scope to transform it into a spacious, modern dwelling.

Above **An elevated bathroom floor creates a storage space underneath.** Top Left **The hatch door doubles as a kitchen table.** Bottom Left **A view through the hatch.** Right **The apartment enjoys high ceilings and plenty of natural light.**

A long, low bench offers open and concealed storage in the living room.

Stendhal

Studio ____ Miogui
Location ____ Paris, France
Square footage ____ 13 m² (140 ft²)

It was a case of déjà vu when Miogui was commissioned to refurbish a tiny apartment in Paris's 20th arrondissement, as the architect had already worked on a very similar studio in the same building.

The result, Miogui says, was "almost the same space, with some differences that create a different plan with the same concept."

To achieve the primary mission of making the space look bigger, the architect stripped the apartment back to its raw elements, removing the existing bathroom to expose the room's second window and installing a small triangular unit in one corner to house the shower room and a tiny kitchen.

For Miogui, consistency in color, form, and materials avoids the jarring notes that can clutter a small space. Here the building's concrete pillars and beams are exposed, the walls painted white, and the kitchen and bookshelves built from pine plywood, with white mosaic tiling for the bathroom.

To maximize space, the architect engaged in a game of perception and abstraction. A mirrored wall reflecting the diagonal pattern of the parquet floor creates the illusion of an identical room next door. And the bathroom door and the curtain that conceals the kitchen blur into each other, both rendered in the same shade of powder blue.

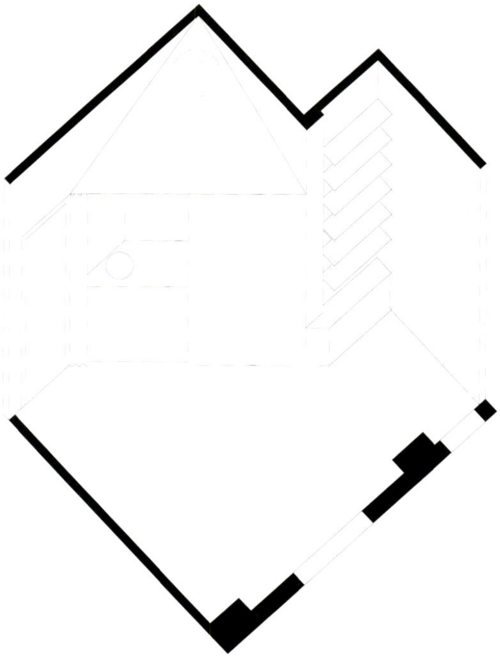

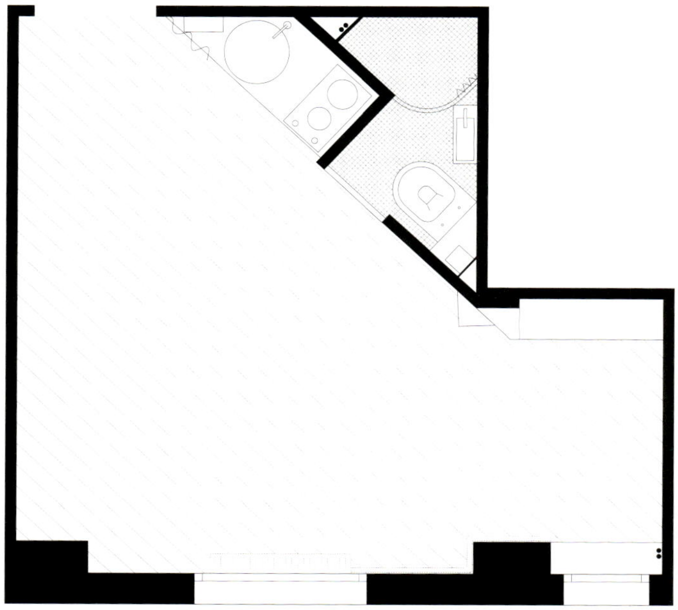

Top Left **A curtain pulls back to reveal the tiny kitchen.** Bottom Left **The apartment plan from the side.** Bottom Right **This bird's-eye view reveals the ingeniously compressed bathroom and kitchen units.** Right **A seamless mirrored wall creates the illusion of space.**

Left **The building's concrete pillars are left exposed.** Right **A mirrored door helps expand the tiny bathroom.**

The architect found beauty and order through geometrical shapes, such as the bathroom's triangular metal roof with circular skylight to draw in natural light, while a mosaic triangle jutting out of the unit serves to conceal some essential pipework and also acts as a plinth for sculptures or plants.

For some practices, the idea of returning to an identical space to solve similar problems might have been off-putting, but not for Miogui. "To work in almost the same space is very interesting as it shows the possibilities are endless," the architect says. "The same concepts of minimalism, compactness, natural light, geometry, beauty of plan, reflections, attention to details, and materials are applied ... for different results."

Studio Vila Olímpia

Studio — Tria Arquitetura
Location — São Paulo, Brazil
Square footage — $27 m^2$ ($290 ft^2$)

For the renovation of a tiny studio in São Paulo, Marina Cardoso de Almeida and Sarah Bonanno of Tria Arquitetura worked to balance both privacy and creativity to design a home that could adapt to a range of residents.

Their first objective was to increase the square footage by incorporating the balcony, which allowed room for a kitchen/dining room next to the windows.

To avoid the bedroom being immediately visible from the apartment's front door, the architects installed the bed inside a sleeping nook, partitioned away from the entrance by an elaborate wall built from perforated concrete bricks.

Creating this barrier between the front door and the bedroom gives privacy to the sleeping zone while still allowing natural light to flow through the gaps. Similarly, the bathroom, formerly separated with just a pane of glass, is given increased privacy with a slatted wooden blind.

Left **An ornate wall of perforated concrete keeps the bedroom private.** Right **A tailor-made piece of furniture incorporates bed and seating bench.**

The whole space features semi-delineated zones—bedroom, kitchen, dining room, living room—connected by a tailor-made piece of wooden furniture that passes through them all, forming the base for the bed and sofa, and serving as a seat and drawer in the kitchen.

Private and public areas are lightly demarcated with Formica, with a wood-grain effect used for the bedroom and bathroom cabinets, while the kitchen units and shelving are painted white.

The architects chose Formica because it harmonizes well with other elements in the design, including the blasted cement wall above the seating area and the sanded bricks in the kitchen. "In small spaces, this is fundamental so as not to further increase the feeling of confinement," explains Marina Cardoso de Almeida.

By incorporating concealed storage in the built-in furniture and designing perforated barriers that allow light to flow, the architects have created a flexible and efficient tiny home.

Left **A wall of sanded bricks brings a flush of color to the white and gray storage cabinets.** Right **The bathroom sink and mirrored cabinet are placed to the rear.**

Tokyo House

Studio ________________ Unemori Architects
Location ________________ Tokyo, Japan
Square footage ________________ 26 m² (280 ft²)

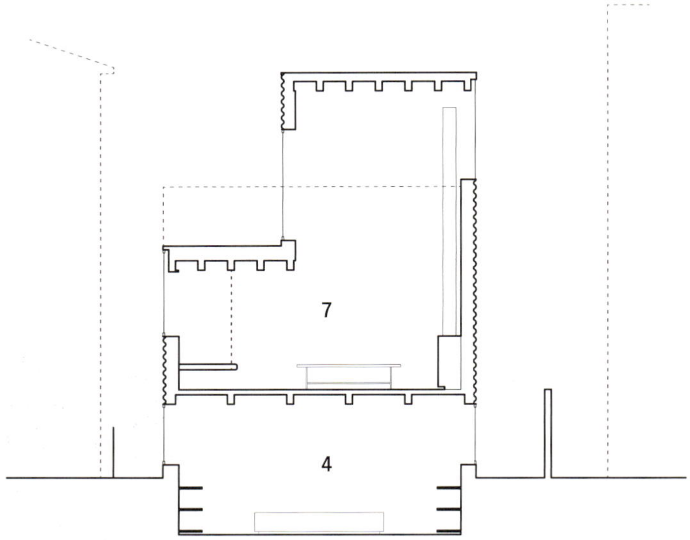

This commission to build a house in one of Tokyo's most densely populated districts came with unusual parameters. Unemori Architects' clients, a couple in their forties, wanted "a temporary abode that would accommodate their near-future plan to return to the countryside," rather than a permanent residence.

The result is a house that embraces a minimalist, pared-back design, offering its inhabitants all the essentials while also inviting them to enjoy the benefits of city life, such as restaurants and public baths, before they relocate to a rural setting.

With the plot positioned in a narrow alleyway, with poor ventilation and little natural light, the architect opted to dig down a few feet to create an enclosed, private semi-basement to house the bedroom, bathroom, and laundry.

Top Left **The semi-basement sits a few feet below ground level.** Bottom Left **Light floods into the space from windows on all sides.** Right **The house was clad in corrugated iron as a nod to its intrinsic impermanence.**

The dining room, living room, office space, and kitchen sit on the floor above, where the ceiling height ranges from 1.9 m (6.2 ft) to a soaring 4.7 m (15.4 ft). Huge windows on all four sides offer views of the street, the neighborhood, and the sky. A ladder leads to a small outdoor space that captures the feeling of freedom and fluidity inherent in the design—described by the architect as "not exactly a roof terrace, but designed to have no specific function."

Constructed from timber on a metal frame, the temporary purpose of the building is denoted in the exposed steel bars, the unvarnished wood, and the corrugated iron that clads the exterior. The architect has paid particular attention to detail with the practicality and elegance of the design, with built-in storage seeming to float over a void and a folded metal staircase leading to the upper level.

For the architect, this house "is really about giving shape to the fluid lifestyle and freedom of the clients, whose wish is to live in this city and leave again to their next destination."

Left **The two levels seen from the door.**
Right **Floating stairs leading up and down.**

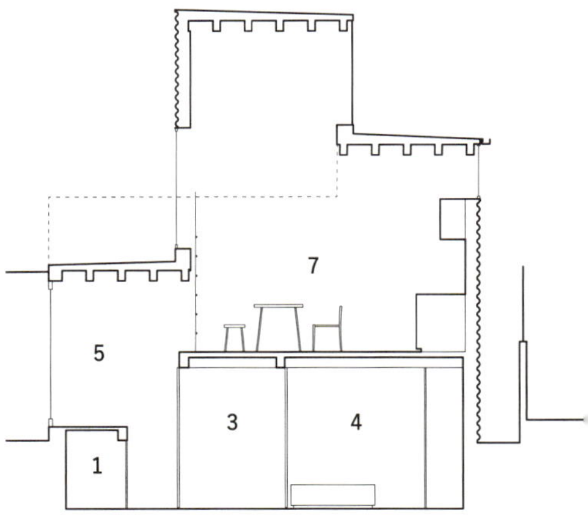

Top **Upstairs are the living room, kitchen, and dining room.** Bottom Left **Multiple windows dot the front facade.** Bottom Right **Plan of the house from the side.** Right **A view over the main living space.**

The Tiniest House

Studio	Aixopluc
Location	Reus, Spain
Square footage	3.2 m² (34 ft²)

"This humble hut is for those who dream about building a house and believe they can't afford it," says Spanish architecture practice Aixopluc, which wanted to find a working solution to the problem of making old or derelict buildings inhabitable without a huge renovation budget.

The answer was a tiny plywood hut with the internal floor space of a queen-sized bed and a cost, including transport and assembly, of €2,320 ($2,375). The studio describes it as "an ambulant family home that can be passed from generation to generation, becoming the relative center of the descendants."

With flexibility—the house can be transformed from a bedroom into a dining area in a few easy steps—and a tiny footprint, it can be erected within empty buildings in the center of the city, and the space is immediately habitable. "By creating a minimal new indoor space, all the existing space is requalified as an in-between, the whole apartment becoming almost like a porch," says Aixopluc.

Top Left **Custom-designed plywood chairs.** Bottom Left **Holes have been perforated on many surfaces to provide a range of hanging options.** Right **Decorative elements such as terrazzo sinks and surfaces break up the plywood.**

All the facilities for other life essentials, such as cooking, bathing, and storage, are outside the house, in units designed by Aixopluc as part of its Homeful modular furniture system. Panels can be configured in different ways to form different rooms, such as a bathroom, kitchen, or storage area. Many have holes where pegs can be slotted in to hang clothes or utensils from.

Consistent with its mission to repurpose abandoned places, Aixopluc has also made an environmentally driven choice in using poplar plywood, which is grown and made close to the architect's studio, thus reducing transportation and ecological costs.

The only thing missing is decoration, a deliberate choice. "The house is bare and raw ... enough to inhabit pleasantly without damaging the environment."

Left **A view from the outside.**
Right **The simple layout incorporates a number of storage solutions.**

Top Left **Seating for six—at least.** Bottom Left **A wood-burning stove.** Right **The A-frame house is designed to fit a queen-sized bed.**

A Guy, a Bulldog, an Edible Garden, and the Home They Share

Studio	Husos
Location	Madrid, Spain
Square footage	46 m^2 (495 ft^2)

Husos's recalibration of a small apartment in a 1960s residential block in Madrid needed to take several specifics into consideration.

The home was designed for an ER doctor and his bulldog, Albóndiga—a breed known to be particularly sensitive to heat. The top priority, therefore, was keeping the apartment, and the dog, cool in the blistering Madrid summers. To facilitate this, the internal walls were removed to create a multipurpose, open-plan living area that allows air to circulate. The architect also designed a collection of moveable cotton pads for Albóndiga to rest on—raised above the ground, they allow cool air to flow underneath the bulldog.

Husos also created a vertical edible garden on the west-facing balcony, which functions as a thermal cushion to help cool the apartment without the need for costly air conditioning. The garden is irrigated using recycled gray water from the shower, a process that can be seen in action via a micro-landscape of tubes and filters hung along the internal wall.

With the client frequently working night shifts, and daytime often set aside for naps, Husos designed a siesta capsule that preserves the bedroom for night-time use. It also acts as a spare bedroom and a reading nook, with light coming in from the periscope window behind the back rest. The sliding door, which can be pulled across for privacy, doubles as a projector screen for TV and movies.

By investigating and reflecting the realities of the client's (and his pet's) daily life, as well as broader climate-based concerns, Husos has built a highly specific dwelling that is responsive to the modern world.

Top **Sliding doors pull across to shield the bedroom.** Bottom **The reading nook's opaque door doubles as a projector screen.**

Left **A periscope window brings light into the reading nook.** Top Right **Light, movable furniture keeps the small space from feeling crowded.** Bottom Right **Clusters of cotton pads allow Albóndiga the bulldog to sleep in comfort with cool air flowing beneath him.**

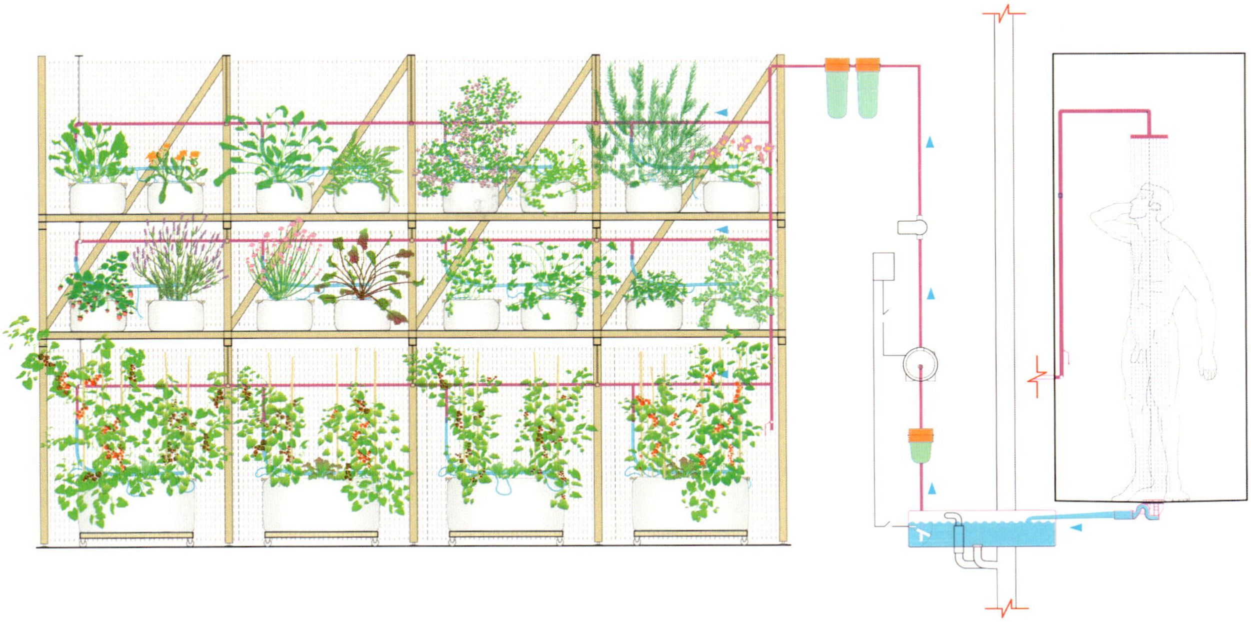

Left **Albóndiga in the balcony garden.** Top Right **The vegetable garden is watered with gray water from the shower.** Bottom Left **The neutral bathroom is enlivened with neon accessories.** Bottom Right **Elements of the irrigation system.**

Left **Soft, colored lighting creates a cozy atmosphere.** Right **A view of the apartment from outside.**

Svätoplukova

Studio ____ Kilo Honč
Location ____ Bratislava, Slovakia
Square footage ____ 67 m² (721 ft²)

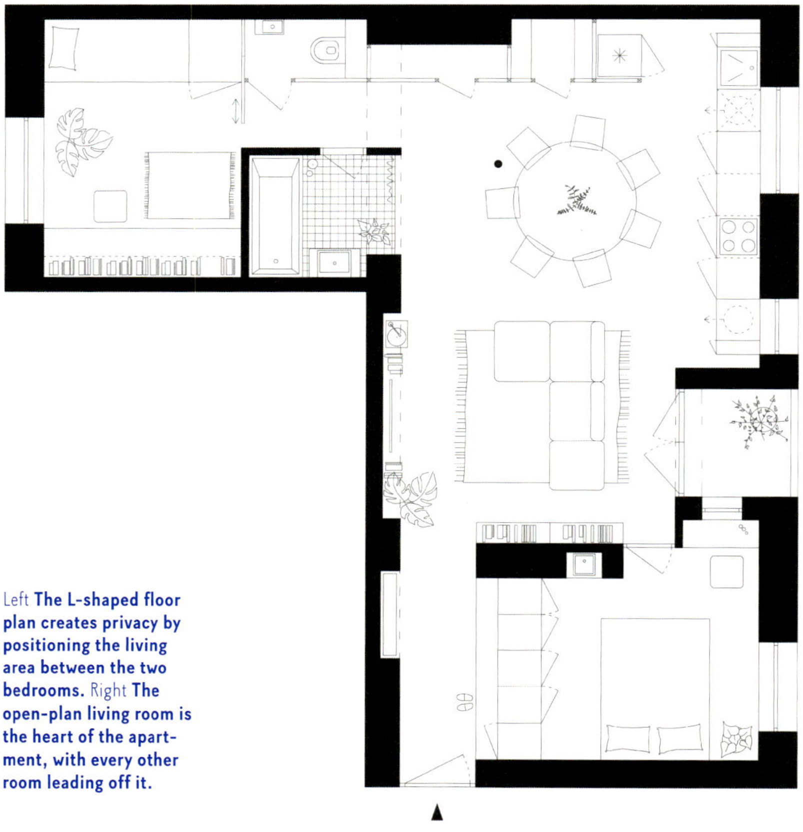

Left **The L-shaped floor plan creates privacy by positioning the living area between the two bedrooms.** Right **The open-plan living room is the heart of the apartment, with every other room leading off it.**

Slovakian architecture practice Kilo Honč transformed a traditional 1950s apartment into an open, functional, and bright family home.

"Our concept opens the apartment up," the architect explains, "in the space, materials, and construction, in height but also in width." By eliminating unnecessary smaller rooms, the new design allows light to enter the central living space, or day zone, from both east and west.

Encompassing the kitchen, living room, and dining area, and connected to all other rooms in the house, the day zone needed to feel spacious and open, but also well defined. A lounging and TV area was positioned near the hallway, while the kitchen units were set against the east wall, with a wall of mirrored storage cabinets set at a 90-degree angle to them, and the six-seater circular dining table in between.

The mirrors stretch west to the main bedroom entrance, creating continuity and providing concealed storage, as well as bringing light through from that side of the apartment.

A glass square containing the white-tiled bathroom overlooks the dining area, a curtain hanging ready to be pulled across for privacy. On the other side, a glass door opens on to the loggia, the apartment's small slice of outside space.

Envisaging a multipurpose space for a young family, the practice designed a home that prioritized social interaction while also allowing for privacy, by positioning the parents' and children's rooms on opposite sides of the apartment. Decoration is pared back, with a sense of informality created by deliberately imperfectly painted walls and surfaces, and the stripped-back ceiling beams and construction poles left standing in the center of the main room.

Mirrored doors illuminate the kitchen / dining area and make it feel more expansive.

DĚTSKÝ DIAPROJEKTOR
A szerelem füveskertje
KÉPES SZÍNHÁZTÖRTÉNET
IDEGEN SZAVAK MAGYARUL
HISTORICKÉ MESTÁ na Slovensku
ZAKÁZANÁ RÉTORIKA
ROZHOVORY S PICASSOM
FRENCH
DO PLAVIEK
'80
OSEMDESIATE

Left **Plexiglas shelves create unobtrusive storage.** Top Right **Tailor-made plywood closets in the bedroom house the client's clothes.** Bottom Right **The unfinished effect adds texture and context to the walls.**

Left **A glass wall allows light to penetrate the bathroom, with a curtain for privacy.** Right **Stripping back the ceiling beams and brickwork creates a connection to the apartment's history.**

Jean Moulin Atelier-House

Studio ____ Atelier NEA
Location ____ Paris, France
Square footage ____ 80 m^2 (861 ft^2)

Situated down a quiet alleyway, this 1940s artist's studio was repurposed by Atelier NEA to create a home for a creative couple who wanted an intimate space that reflected their personalities. The design combined the original elements of the structure, with its huge windows stretching up to a skylight in the roof, and a radical recalibration of the layout.

Fundamental to the change was moving the two staircases from the back of the house to the front—a shift that maintained the double-height space at the building's core while creating distinct levels that become more private further up the structure.

The ground floor houses the kitchen, living space, working area, and most of the storage, while remaining fundamentally flexible and capable of adapting to accommodate any purpose.

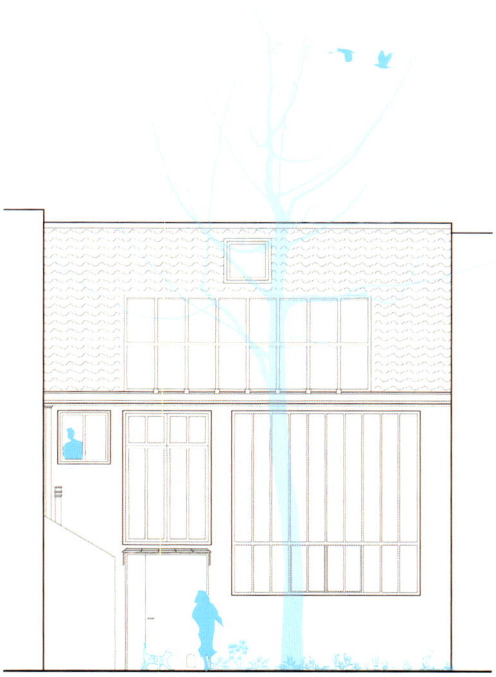

Left **A facade full of windows.** Right **A second-floor landing doubles as a study.**

The house overlooks the residence's private terrace and an old maple tree, a feature echoed in the sycamore maple wood used to construct the integral structures of the house.

Atelier NEA's ambition was to use raw and light materials to minimize the need for additional furniture, which might overpower

the small space. The solution was nearly two dozen custom-made sycamore maple and steel built-in units that slot together harmoniously to form the kitchen, sleeping nooks, walk-in closets, towering shelving units, and sliding doors, as well as forming the framework for the house itself. Using porous materials, such as jute for the doors and perforated steel for the walk-in closet, the design ensures privacy while allowing natural light through. A color palette of pale wood and white paint, waxed concrete and gray-flecked Carrara marble keeps the internal energy of the space calm, creating the perfect setting for the owners to enhance with their own personalities and passions.

Left **The serene kitchen is built in sycamore maple joinery with marble tops.**
Right **The plans of the house's three floors.**
Top Right **Light metal stairs allow space for continuous storage on the ground floor.**
Bottom Right **A view of the landing.**

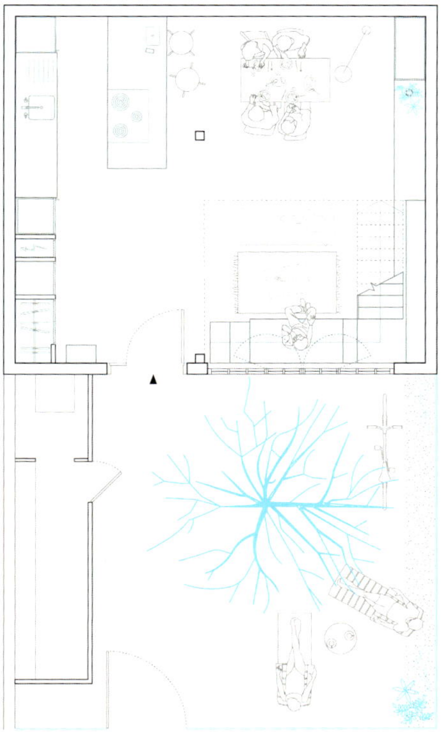

Ground floor

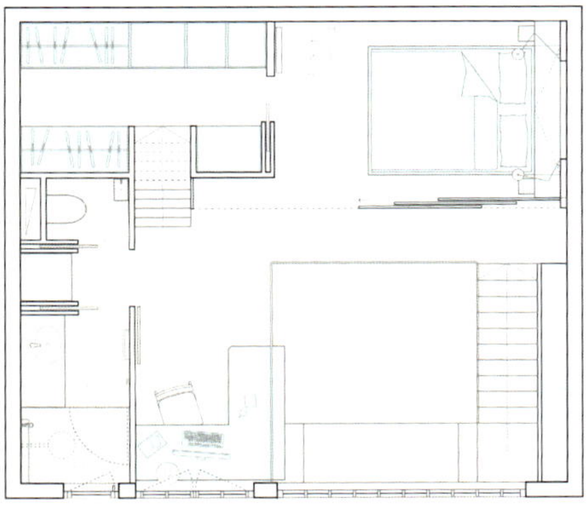

First floor

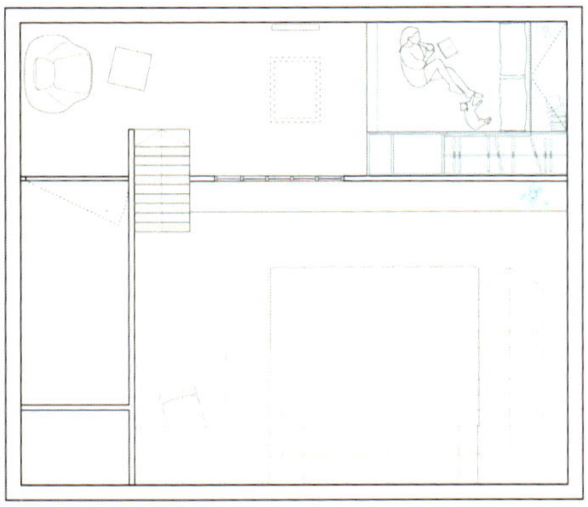

2nd floor

La Nave

Studio	Nomos
Location	Madrid, Spain
Square footage	227 m^2 (2,442 ft^2)

The transformation of a former print shop in Madrid was a very personal project for two members of the Nomos team, as La Nave would become their family home.

Making the shift from an open-plan industrial layout to a domestic structure required a complete recalibration of the space. The initial idea of positioning the apartment's enclosed rooms and wet areas at the rear had to be abandoned because the existing plumbing was attached to the house's central concrete columns. This meant that the wet areas had to be placed centrally instead.

Nomos worked around this by positioning the wet areas and enclosed rooms in line with the central columns, but at a 45-degree angle to the outer walls, drawing natural light deep into the house while creating a sequence of well-defined spaces that flow in a continuous loop.

Top Left **A glass-lined corridor, or winter garden, acts as a cushion between the house and street outside.** Bottom Left **Furniture has been chosen to fit into the 45-degree spaces created by the layout.** Right **The winter garden doubles as a children's play area.**

The kitchen countertops are made from repurposed terrazzo flooring.

Left **Storage units employ ruched green curtains instead of doors.** Right **Narrow shelves in the kitchen hold architectural maquettes.** Above Top **A cacophony of colored tiles and cut plywood creates the house's eclectic decoration.** Above Bottom **Bunk beds sit in a nook.**

Left **The main suite uses frosted glass in the bathroom and curtains in the bedroom to achieve privacy.** Right **The brick tiles continue downwards to surround the bath.**

Partitions in brick and MDF panels jut out from the central columns in a joyous zigzag formation. Constructed from glazed bricks in terra-cotta, white, and cobalt blue on pine frames, they achieve a combination of solidity and lightness that adds to the spaciousness of the home, as well as being inherently decorative.

The architect used the materials to inform the design, stating that "the vertically placed bricks generate plinths, shelves, and friezes; in combination with large, hollow brick boards, they define niches and shelves." Most of the fixtures were custom-made by Nomos, including a curved kitchen island made from old terrazzo flooring that was repurposed from the apartment's former commercial life.

Along the wall of windows forming what had once been the printshop's facade, Nomos created a glass-lined corridor, or winter garden, that acts as a thermal buffer and cushion between the private domain and the world outside. "The winter garden is the apartment's living center," says Nomos, "shaping the sensory experience, graduating its intimacy, and nuancing its light."

Complete Transformation for an Apartment

Studio ______ Pierre-Louis Gerlier
Location ______ Paris, France
Square footage ______ 32 m² (344 ft²)

A couple who lives mostly in the countryside wanted a "cocoon" in Paris for their infrequent visits to the city. They commissioned architect Pierre-Louis Gerlier to transform an unloved apartment in a 19th-century building in Saint-Germain-des-Prés into a bright space that felt like "a hotel, with simple and pure decoration."

The apartment's location on the second floor overlooking a courtyard meant it was quite dark, so the architect's primary objective was to fill the space with light. To achieve this, the layout was reorganized, with all the utilities, the bathroom, and the shower room placed behind a curved wall that hugs the back of the space.

"Curves are a good way to fluidize small spaces," says Gerlier, and ribbed oak paneling adds warmth and a decorative element

without overpowering the room. The shower room and bathroom are made cozy and intimate with their dark-green waxed concrete walls, which contrast with the bright white of the public spaces and the apple-green detailing on the bed frame, the kitchen cupboards, and the desk.

To align with the clients' brief that the room should feel like a luxury hotel, many of the familiar essentials of modern living—such

Left **All the functional elements of the house are concealed behind a rippling curved screen.** Right **The architect maximized the small square footage by creating a fully open-plan space.**

as innovative storage solutions or high-tech kitchen equipment—are dispensed with almost completely. A slim closet is positioned between the entry door and the desk, while the kitchen features just a sink and a small stovetop. "The occupants take advantage of their stay in Paris to go to restaurants," explains Gerlier. This restraint is echoed in the unassuming decoration, which maximizes the apartment's tiny square-footage through a pared-back color palette and minimal furniture. The result is, as the architect describes, "a nice balance between tradition and modernity by using noble materials in a contemporary design."

Yona Friedman / Pro Domo

Left **The all-white color scheme is invigorated by the furniture's bright hues.** Right **A large mirror over the desk reflects the space and makes it seem larger.**

Yona Friedman / Pro Domo

Yona Friedman / Pro Domo

Top Left **As per the client's instructions, the kitchen holds just the essentials.** Bottom Left **The chosen furniture is as flexible as the space itself.** Right **Concealed cabinets sit opposite the entrance door.**

Smart Zendo

Studio — Sim-Plex
Location — Coastal Skyline, Hong Kong
Square footage — 46 m² (492 ft²)

Sim-Plex was commissioned by a family of three to redesign a small urban apartment near the Hong Kong airport to create a space that combined intelligent devices with the ancient traditions of feng shui, while incorporating natural materials from the surrounding landscape.

"The spirit of Zen is the pursuit of harmony," explains the architect. "The Smart Zendo is based on the spiritual details of Zen." The ambition was to build a harmonious living space that uses ingenious storage solutions and labor-minimizing technology to turn a home into a sanctuary.

In the family, both parents frequently travel for work, so the grandmother comes to look after their son, but the original apartment had no place for her to sleep. Sim-Plex's new layout transformed the main room into a flexible space that can be reconfigured in different ways including, through concealed sliding doors, into a third bedroom.

The installation of a wooden deck in the living room allows the floor to double as storage, with compartments in the platform accessed by pull-up doors. By the window, an electronic coffee table rises on demand from the floor (and just as seamlessly disappears), providing a spot for working or tea ceremonies that makes the most of the apartment's extraordinary views.

Both bedrooms prioritize storage. A vanity mirror is concealed in a drawer next to the main bed, while the integrated drawers in the son's room double as a desk chair. But the space isn't just functional—the wooden window frames also reference the feng shui principle of balance, using a natural material to offset the technology elsewhere.

Hardware such as voice-activated synthesizers, electronic clothes hangers, an electronic table, a smart toilet, and multiple televisions define the modernity of the space but never to the exclusion of the world outside.

"Although the traditional feng shui aesthetics and smart technology seem to be contradictory," Sim-Plex says, "if applied properly, they have their compatibility."

Left **Almost every surface, including the floor, incorporates storage.** Right **The curved bench and stool fit seamlessly under the kitchen counter.**

Left **A smart coffee table rises from floor level to offer a space for the tea ceremony.** Top Right **The bedroom enjoys both extensive storage and light.** Bottom Right **Marble walls bring a touch of luxury to the bathroom.**

Left **A study-cum-lounge area.**
Top Right **A platform of raised storage also works as the desk seating.**
Bottom Right **The bed has extraordinary views over the Hong Kong hills.**

CUPA Housing Renovation

Studio ______ Escobedo Soliz
Location ______ Mexico City, Mexico
Square footage ______ 55 m² (592 ft²)

An opportunity to renovate an apartment in the CUPA housing project—Centro Urbano Presidente Alemán—offered architect Escobedo Soliz the chance to reimagine an interior in Mexico's first modernist residential complex.

CUPA was commissioned by the state in 1947 to address a growing demand for housing in Mexico City. Architect Mario Pani took just two years to build the complex, constructing 1,080 apartments across six high-rise and six low-rise buildings in a "super block," with the buildings' footprint occupying roughly 30% of the block's total area.

Inspired by the principles of Le Corbusier's Radiant City—setting urban tower blocks among extensive green space—the project also established social infrastructure for inhabitants such as sports facilities, commercial spaces, and schools.

The clients had lived in their duplex apartment for 15 years, and it showed. They wanted more privacy and storage, separate bedrooms for parents and sons, as well as functional improvements to bring ease and flow to the home.

The redesign shortened and steepened the staircase, creating space underneath for a TV room. A large piece of custom-built

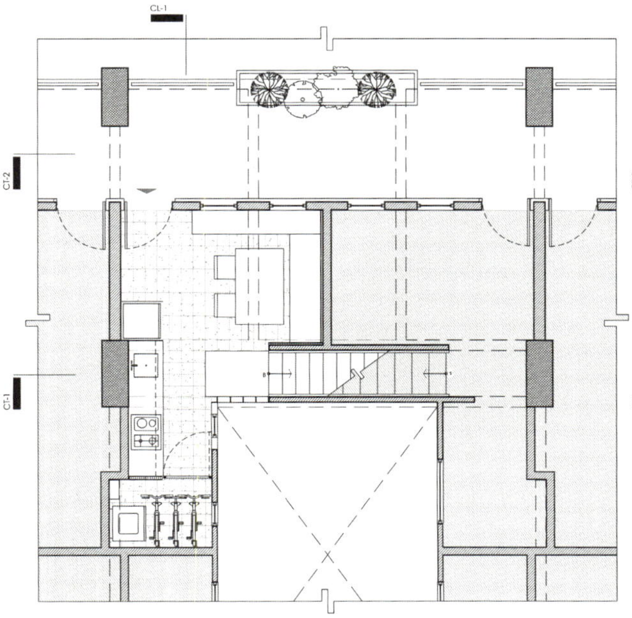

LEVEL 0

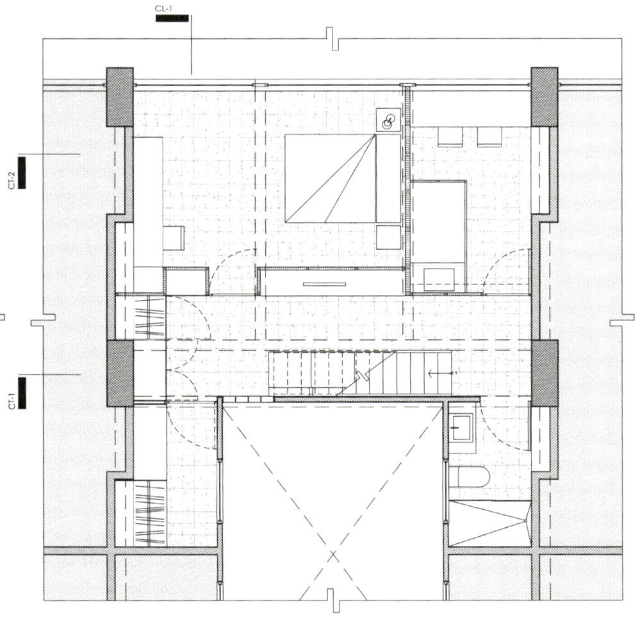

LEVEL -1

Top Left **Interior courtyard at the housing project.** Bottom Left **The new layout for both floors of the duplex apartment.** Right **The floating staircase created space for additional storage and a sofa for watching TV.**

cabinetry was inserted to elegantly divide the lower floor into separate zones, while also providing closet space, storage units, desks, and a bunk bed.

The building's existing framework of concrete beams and columns was stripped back and left exposed to complement the golden wood furniture and white terrazzo floors. By leaving gaps between the beams and partitions, the design ensures light can penetrate right to the center of the apartment.

As well as recognizing the need for modernization, Escobedo Soliz wanted to stay true to the fabric and intention of the building, and so used the same design for built-in storage that had been proposed in 1947 by Cuban-born furniture designer Clara Porset.

Left **Built-in closets, shelves, and a desk improved the functionality of the bedrooms.** Top Right **The cabinetry and the partition walls are all constructed in the same wood.** Bottom Right **Gaps between walls and ceiling let light flow into the inner parts of the house.**

Left The floors and kitchen countertops are covered in a light terrazzo. Right Shortening the staircase created extra room for a dining nook by the kitchen.

Lightbox—Increase Light in All Spaces

Studio ______ studiobravo
Location ______ Paris, France
Square footage ______ 42 m² (452 ft²)

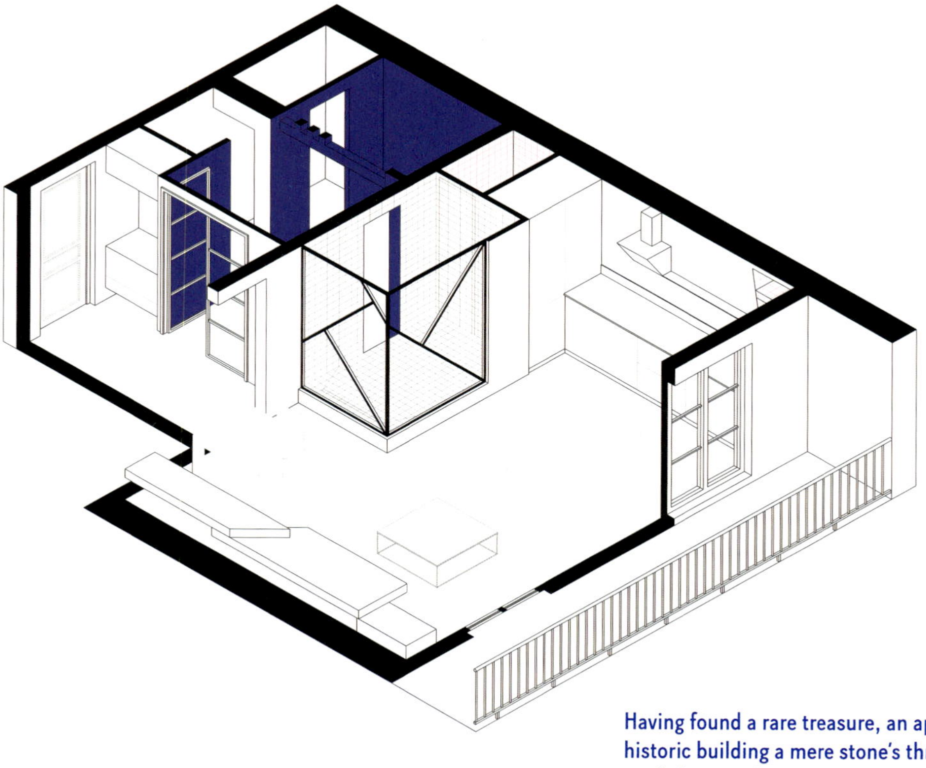

Having found a rare treasure, an apartment with a balcony in a historic building a mere stone's throw from the Opéra Garnier, studiobravo's client wanted to renovate the space into a contemporary haven full of natural light.

Central to the brief was the creation of a large, open-plan living space with direct access to the balcony. Realizing this ambition required the complete reconfiguration of the layout, moving the kitchen into the living room, and repositioning the bedroom, painted a rich blue that looks vibrant even in low light, at the rear to create a restful cocoon.

Left **The plan demonstrates the built-in elements of the design.** Right **A view across the open-plan living room toward the kitchen.**

The result, after the partition walls came down and a sleek integrated kitchen was repositioned against the wall, was a light, airy space, subtly separated into sitting, lounging, working, and eating zones, with a tiled alcove above a multifunctional bench that can be used as a sofa or a single bed. Additionally, studiobravo custom-designed a movable kitchen island to provide extra preparation space as well as to act as an informal, flexible room divider.

To retain the spacious feel in the main area, most of the storage units are found at the back. A closet and laundry are situated off the bedroom, and there is a storage for coats and shoes by the front door.

Maximizing light was all-important, as the apartment only had two windows at the front, plus a small skylight. A solution was found in the design of the ribbed-glass and galvanized-steel bathroom, which filters sunlight through to the bedroom by day and acts as a dramatic lightbox by night, illuminating and energizing the living room while retaining privacy.

The architect's design philosophy celebrates the energy and possibilities of the urban environment, so for studiobravo, "developing comfortable, enjoyable, and affordable tiny living spaces is critical to maintaining social diversity in today's largest cities."

Left **A cork wall runs the length of the entrance hallway, creating scope for ever changing decoration.** Top Right **A glass door leads to the bedroom painted Yves Klein blue.** Bottom Right **The white tiled shower room expands into the living room with a frosted glass box.**

Top Left **An elongated wall lamp illuminates the dining table.** Bottom Left **An asymmetric wall nook offers storage over the sink.** Right **The custom-designed sofa bench can transform into a spare bed.**

ELU Sapfous

Studio ___ Bare Space
Location ___ Athens, Greece
Square footage ___ 25 m^2 (270 ft^2) per apartment

Greece-based architect Bare Space was commissioned to convert a series of office and industrial buildings into sustainable and inexpensive micro-housing.

The question the practice asked was, "How can we create consistently high-standard living conditions in small apartments in different existing shells?" The solution was to design three Essential Living Units (ELUs), one each for sleeping, eating, and washing, which can be inserted in a variety of configurations into small spaces to maximize their potential.

The pilot building was a former industrial property in Kallithea, Attica, one of Athens's most densely populated districts. The architect wanted to maintain the historic fabric of the building and minimize structural interventions, except to improve energy efficiency and insulation, when creating the 25 micro-apartments.

Several communal areas are included in the design—a laundry, bike racks, and storage lockers downstairs, plus a generous terrace on the roof—meaning that the units themselves can be optimized for living pleasurably, rather than, for example, storage.

Taking inspiration from train and yacht cabins, the ELUs are distinct designs that work together "like Lego blocks." The sleeping cabin comprises a bed on a platform behind a screen, with a curved window obscured by a curtain. In taller rooms, it has a ladder leading

Left **The sleeping block surrounds the bed with a range of storage options from shelves to closets to drawers.** Right **A shallow alcove in the bedroom is designed to hold an alarm clock, a phone, or a glass of water.**

up to a mezzanine with space for storage or a second bed; in less lofty rooms it has built-in closets. The kitchen is a fully integrated block with a fridge, oven, sink, and stovetop, as well as lots of storage, while the bathroom is a simple cube with shower, sink, and toilet. Consistency is created by using pale wood and seamless joinery, with all the materials—flaxseed floors, natural stone wool insulation, and wood—chosen for their low environmental impact.

The process is ongoing. "The system is constantly evolving," the architect says. "The goal is to continuously improve the product provided."

Top Left **The floor plan shows how the Essential Living Units (ELUs) can be used in multiple configurations.**
Bottom Left **The former industrial building has been refreshed but otherwise left largely unchanged.**
Top Right **The fully integrated kitchen unit holds all the essential washing, cooking, and refrigeration appliances.**
Bottom Right **Bare Space took inspiration from train cabin design to create the bedroom units.**

Left **A neutral palette helps create an uncluttered feel in a small space.**
Top Right **Integrated storage elsewhere allows the desk area to be less defined.**
Bottom Right **A curtain allows privacy in the bedroom area.**

La Tournette

Studio ______ Freaks
Location ______ Paris, France
Square footage ______ 30 m² (323 ft²)

Two retired architects who spend their weekdays in the country and weekends in Paris asked architecture practice Freaks to convert a glass-fronted former workshop into the perfect pied-à-terre.

With the apartment covering just 30 m² (323 ft²) and a brief that asked for flexibility, room for entertaining, space to work, and occasional accommodation for their two adult daughters, the practice drew inspiration from the theater to build a pivotal structure that could be reconfigured in a variety of ways.

Freaks constructed La Tournette, named after the revolving stage that allows a theatrical company to seamlessly change the scenery. It is a "large, monolithic, and sculptural mobile cupboard," incorporating shelves and a folding table, that organizes the space in many configurations depending on where it is positioned.

D-shaped and bright white, the structure is formed completely of cubed shelves on one side, while the other side is smooth except for a hidden table that folds out from the center to provide seating for four. Set on wheels, the object can be positioned anywhere in the open-plan space, either in the middle, to shield the kitchen and mezzanine, or pushed to the side to leave the space free for work or parties.

The private areas of the house sit in a block to the rear and comprise a bathroom tiled in white with black grouting, a walk-in closet, and a fully integrated kitchen with glossy white cabinetry. On the top, accessed by a wall-mounted ladder, is the sleeping mezzanine, which can be made private by repositioning the arched mobile unit.

The workshop's original fluted windows keep the space light yet private, and sustain the feeling of the apartment's creative past—an energy that continues in the flow and flexibility of La Tournette's spinning central structure.

Left **The view from the street.** Top Right **The space has dozens of permutations, thanks to La Tournette, a custom-built "mobile cupboard."** Bottom Right **The former workshop's wall of glass provides the apartment's source of natural light.**

Top Left **A wall-mounted ladder on the right provides access to the mezzanine.** Bottom Left **The sleeping mezzanine is above the kitchen.** Bottom Right **The tiny bathroom is kept bright with square white tiles.** Right **The kitchen is paneled in glossy white to luminous effect.**

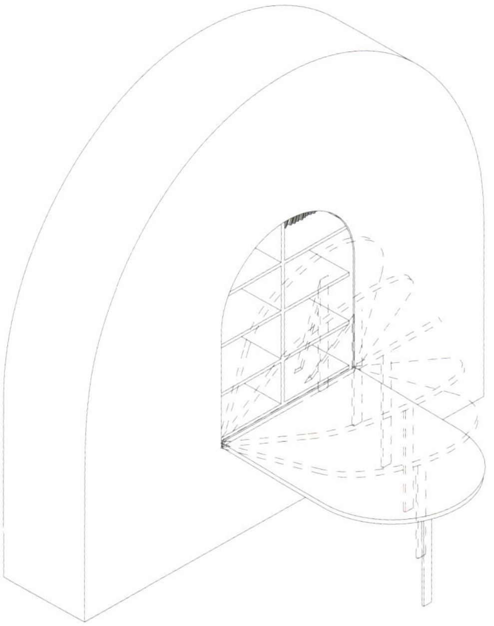

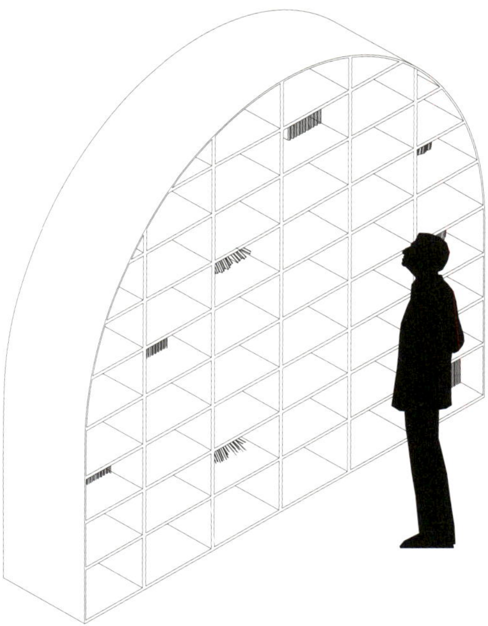

Top Left **The cupboard's central panel folds down to form a dining table and desk.** Bottom Left **The back of the unit is a mosaic of storage shelves.** Right **The walls of the apartment have been left bare, to increase spaciousness.**

Index

Kilo Honč
www.kilohonc.com
Svätoplukova
pp. 20 (bottom), 42 (top), 198–205
Photography Matej Hakár

Louis Denavaut
www.louisdenavaut.com
Saint-Roch Duplex
pp. 150–157
Photography Christophe Coënon

Agence Marn Déco
www.marn-deco.com
Studette Neuilly-Plaisance
p. 35
Studette
pp. 50–53
Photography BCDF Studio—Bertrand Fompeyrine

Max Enrich and Diana Martin's House
www.maxenrich.com
pp. 18–19
Photography Never Too Small

Miogui
www.mioguiarchitecture.fr
Stendhal
pp. 170–173
Photography Philippe Billard

Nicholas Gurney
www.nicholasgurney.com.au
The Warren
pp. 84–91
Photography Michael Wee

Nicolas Bossard Architecture
www.instagram.com/nicolasbossardarchitecture
Villa Saint-Michel
pp. 54–57
Photography BCDF Studio—Bertrand Fompeyrine

Nomos
www.nomos.archi
La Nave
pp. 25, 210–217
Photography Luis Asín

Mistovia
www.mistovia.com
AFR Koszutka
pp. 2, 158–163
Photography ONI Studio

Otherside Objects, Sam Klemic
www.othersideobjects.com
Sam Klemick's work/home studio
pp. 44, 46
Photography Ye Rin Mok

Pierre-Louis Gerlier
www.pierrelouisgerlier.com
Complete Transformation for an Apartment
pp. 218–223
Photography Ercole Salinaro

Proctor & Shaw
www.proctorandshaw.com
Shoji Apartment
pp. 4, 130–133
Photography Ståle Eriksen

Sim-Plex
www.sim-plex-design.com
Smart Zendo
pp. 24, 28, 47, 224–229
Photography Patrick Lam

studiobravo
www.studiobravo.archi
Lightbox—Increase Light in All Spaces
pp. 236–241
Photography Bertrand Noël

Studiomama
www.studiomama.com
13 m² House
p. 49 (top)
Photography Rei Moon

Tenhachi Architect and Interior Design
www.ten-hachi.com
Tenhachi House
pp. 6 (bottom), 26–27
Photography Akihide Mishima

Tria Arquitetura
www.triaarquitetura.com.br
Studio Vila Olímpia
pp. 174–177
Photography Alessandro Guimarães

Unemori Architects
www.unemori-archi.com
Tokyo House
pp. 178–183
Photography Kai Nakamura

Yuichi Yoshida & Associates
www.4sdy1.com
Tsukiji Room H
pp. 36, 126–129
Photography Katsumi Hirabayashi

YUUA
www.yuua.jp
1.8 m Width House
pp. 12–13
Photography Toshihiro Sobajima

Zyva Studio
www.zyvastudio.com
Straight Curves Apartment
pp. 14 (top), 138–143
Photography Valentin Fougeray

Pretty Small

Grand Living with Limited Space

This book was conceived, edited, and designed by gestalten.

Edited by Robert Klanten and Laura Allsop

Introduction, project texts, and captions by Letitia Wrigley
Feature texts by Letitia Wrigley: pp. 10–15, 30–49;
Alisa Kotmair: pp. 16–29

Editorial Management by Anastasia Buryak

Creative Direction of Design by Ludwig Wendt
Layout and cover design: Melanie Ullrich
Photo Editor: Francesca Zoe Paterniani

Typefaces: Baton by Anton Koovit & Yassin Baggar,
Century Old Style by Linn Boyd Benton & Morris Fuller Benton

Cover image: Svätoplukova. Photography Matej Hakár

Back cover: A Guy, a Bulldog, an Edible Garden, and the Home They Share, photography José Hevia; Saint-Roch Duplex, photography Christophe Coënon; Smart Zendo, photography Patrick Lam; The Tiniest House, photography José Hevia

Printed by Printer Trento s.r.l., Trento, Italy
Made in Europe

Published by gestalten, Berlin 2022
ISBN 978-3-96704-077-7

For more information, and to order books, please visit www.gestalten.com

Bibliographic information published by the Deutsche Nationalbibliothek. The Deutsche Nationalbibliothek lists this publication in the Deutsche Nationalbibliografie; detailed bibliographic data is available online at www.dnb.de

MIX
Paper from responsible sources
FSC® C015829
www.fsc.org

This book was printed on paper certified according to the standards of the FSC®.